THE APOCRYPHA, BRIDGE OF THE TESTAMENTS

A Reader's Guide to the Apocryphal Books of the Old Testament

BY ROBERT C. DENTAN

THE SEABURY PRESS · NEW YORK

First Seabury Paperback *revised edition published 1964*
Second Printing 1969

PREFACE

This book is intended to be a guide for the ordinary reader whose attention has been attracted to the section of the Bible called Apocrypha and who desires to know more precisely what it is, why it is important, and how best to go about reading it. Since the book is intended for the general reader, no attempt has been made to offer original solutions to any of the numerous literary and historical problems with which the apocryphal literature abounds, but rather to present the consensus of contemporary scholarship in so far as it can be discovered. Where there are important differences of opinion the fact has usually been noted.

The practical purpose for which this volume is intended has dictated the order in which the books are discussed. They are arranged according to an ascending scale of difficulty and popular appeal so that the book can serve as an easy guide for a program of reading. It is hoped the book will be used for this purpose and not merely as a source of information *about* the Apocrypha. Anyone who makes use of it in this way will find that, after reading two chapters containing essential background facts, he will be introduced first of all to the interesting stories of Daniel, I Esdras,

Tobit, and Judith. These narratives should encourage him to go on to the more demanding but no less rewarding historical and philosophical literature—with the very difficult Esdras apocalypse left to the last. Suggestions are given as to sections which may be omitted without serious loss or which may at least be postponed for a second reading.

The title of the book is not meant to suggest the Apocrypha is a complete bridge over the inter-testamental period, or that there is no other bridge. It merely shows the approximate chronological relationship of the Apocrypha to the two Testaments and suggests the importance of the apocryphal literature in understanding the development of thought and events in the intervening period.

Bible quotations and the form of proper names are generally taken from the King James version, since that will be the version readily available to most readers. It is quite satisfactory for ordinary use, although the Revised Version is in many places more accurate and its style more readable.

While the chief emphasis has been, of necessity, placed on the literary and historical importance of the Apocrypha, the individual reader should find in studying it, with such assistance as is here provided, nourishment for his soul as well as for his mind. The Apocrypha deals with many things which are of direct concern to the spiritual life and has much to say which can contribute to deepening our understanding of God and His wonderful ways. As must be true in studying any other part of the Bible, our ultimate purpose here is to learn about God and not just about books.

Robert C. Dentan

TABLE

OF

CONTENTS

To John Heuss

WHAT
1 | # THE APOCRYPHA
IS

What Is the Value of the Apocrypha? No one deliberately buys a book with a missing section, even though defective copies are sometimes accidentally sold in book stores. If we have ever purchased one, we remember the vexation we felt on first noticing that the last sentence on a certain left-hand page did not continue on the right and that the numbering of the pages suddenly leaped from, say, 128 to 145! If no other copy was available we may have had to continue reading the imperfect one and probably found we could guess the content of the missing section. The absence of a few pages need not necessarily be disastrous, but no one regards such a book as satisfactory and no sane person intentionally buys a copy of an ordinary book he knows to be incomplete.

A Bible without an Apocrypha is very much like a book with a missing section. The omission is not fatal, since the Church (i.e. the Episcopal Church) tells us that no essential point of doctrine is affected (Article Six of the Thirty-nine Articles), and the main course of the Biblical narrative is clear even without the apocryphal books. But it is still a fact that a Bible without an Apocrypha is an incomplete Bible and there is a considerable gap in the story which it tells. It is important to realize just how large that gap is. The last events explicitly recorded in the Old Testament took place during the second governorship of Nehemiah about 433 B.C. (*Neh.* 13: 4-31). Even if we believe, with many scholars, that Ezra (*Ezra* 7-10) really came after Nehemiah instead of being his contemporary, that fact would bring Old Testament history down only to about 398 B.C. The New Testament story does not begin until somewhere around the year 1 of the Christian Era, so by the most conservative estimate the gap in the Bible story covers nearly four hundred years—no inconsiderable period in the life of any people! Besides the break in the continuity of the story, there is an equally important gap in the literature. It is not entirely certain just which of the Old Testament books was the last to be written, but Daniel is a pretty good candidate for the honor and can be dated with certainty in the year 165 B.C. Esther may have been written a little later in the same century, but of that we cannot be entirely sure. In any event, almost two hundred years separate the writing of the latest book of the Old Testament from the first book of the New Testament—probably First Thessalonians, written about A.D. 50.

Anyone who is seriously interested in studying the Bible will want to know what happened during those long, apparently silent, years. He knows, from a general reading of history and his personal experience of the relentless march of events, that neither time nor thought was standing still. These were without doubt the greatest years in the history of the ancient world. It was shortly after the close of Old Testament history that Alexander the Great conquered the East and established Greek civilization everywhere, laying the foundations of a heritage of art, philosophy, and culture which still is ours today. The fact that the New Testament is written in Greek insead of Hebrew or Aramaic is standing witness to the success of Alexander's campaigns, and yet even the later literature of the canonical Old Testament contains no unambiguous reference to him.

After the Greeks, the Romans came. The lands of the Bible, which had been ruled successively by Egypt, Assyria, and Babylonia, and then by Persia and Greece, now became part of the vast empire of Rome. She is the mother of us all in politics and law and yet her name never appears in the canonical Old Testament. Our Bible, which tells us so much about the conquests of Sennacherib and Nebuchadnezzar, seems to contain not even a hint or foreboding of the advent of the Romans.

Those years when Palestine was ruled successively by Greece and Rome largely determined the character of life in the New Testament age. They were marked by obvious changes in political administration, language and manners, and by quiet, but revolutionary, alterations in inherited ways of thought and in religious ideas. When we move from the Old Testament to the New, we are conscious that the two books belong to different worlds, so different that we may doubt that they are really very closely connected.

3

Much of that sense of strangeness arises simply because of the gap of four hundred years in history and two hundred years in literary development which separates the two Testaments. If we wish to understand the world in which Jesus and His disciples moved, we must know something of the troubled times which preceded and created it.

But where can we turn for knowledge? The two principal sources are the writings of the Jewish historian Josephus (c. A.D. 37-95) and the Apocrypha of the Old Testament. Clergy and informed lay people of a former generation usually had copies of Josephus' *Jewish War* and *Antiquities of the Jews* on their shelves, for they could read there not only the story of the inter-testamental period, but also the history of the Herods, the period of the Roman procurators, and the War with Rome. Unfortunately, it would be a counsel of perfection to expect the ordinary layman, or the average clergyman, to read the crowded and interminable pages of Josephus today. For his invaluable account of the period from the rise of the later Hasmoneans to the Fall of Jerusalem, the average reader will have to depend on modern writers who have read his books and have reduced the story to more manageable form. But for the earlier part of the history every reader should have available Josephus' own primary source, I Maccabees, and the other books of the Apocrypha of the Old Testament, which are properly an integral part of the Christian Bible.

While the Apocrypha by no means fills in all the gap between the Testaments, it helps enormously in making it narrower. One who wishes to pass from the Old Testament to the New will find the trip a much smoother one if he travels the interesting route which leads over this most useful bridge. To change the metaphor, one may say that the various books of the Apocrypha can act as guides to conduct the traveler to the other side of the chasm. The Wisdom of Solomon will show him the road which leads from the prophets of ancient Israel to the Gospel of John and the New Testament epistles. The delightful little book of Tobit will introduce him to the kind of home in which Jesus lived and the kind of people who gladly listened to Him. Second Esdras, wild and fantastic as it may seem (though no more so than the book of Revelation!), will give him a deeper understanding of that strange way of thinking called "apocalyptic" which also appears in the closing chapters of Daniel and which influenced so profoundly the minds of men in our Lord's generation. Ecclesiasticus will help him follow the line of development which leads from the "wise men" of the Old Testament to the "scribes" of the New; and the two books of Maccabees will guide him through the most significant and memorable crisis of the intervening period—the heroic struggle of the Jews against the pagan forces that threatened to deprive them of their God and their religion, a struggle which was decisively important in forming the character of the Jewish people in New Testament times.

What Is the Apocrypha? It is not difficult to define the Old or New Testaments. The Old Testament is a collection of the principal works of Hebrew antiquity and has canonical authority for us because the Hebrews were the race through which God chose to work for the redemption of mankind.[1] The New Testament is a collection of the most significant books produced in the first century or so of the Church's existence. They are authoritative because they record the great events which accomplished our salvation and tell of the establishment of the Church, by which the fruits of that salvation were transmitted to later generations. But the Apocrypha cannot be defined so concisely; at any rate it cannot be defined without pausing for some brief preliminary discussion. A definition of it depends upon our knowing something about the Septuagint, the Greek translation of the Old Testament. The story of the Septuagint, itself, belongs to the inter-testamental period, and it is to that story we now must turn our attention.

In the years which followed the end of the Babylonian Exile (538 B.C.), a movement was going on which was destined to take the Jews into every part of the civilized world. Palestine was a poor country. To begin with, it had few natural resources, and the Jews in that period were confined to the least productive part of the land—the little area in the central highlands which surrounded the capital city of Jerusalem. The South belonged to the Edomites (or Idumeans, as they came to be called), and the more desirable region immediately north of Jerusalem was held by the Samaritans, a people basically of the same race and

[1] Canonical means prescribed by authority of the church. The canon of Scripture is a list of the books which the Church (either Christian or Jewish) regards as inspired and authoritative.

religion as the Jews but a people who became, in the course of post-exilic history, the inveterate foes of the Jews.

Surrounded on three sides by foreigners and enemies, and on the fourth by the desolate Jordan valley, the Jewish community seemed to have no prospect of expanding its meager territory. The political liberties of the Jews had been lost first to the Babylonians and then to the Persians and Greeks, so that it was only natural for the prevailing mood in Palestinian Judaism to be one of intense pessimism, at least as far as worldly possibilities were concerned. Under the circumstances, it is not surprising that the pressure of an expanding population caused the younger and more vigorous Jews to seek a better life by emigrating to the great cities of the pagan world. The result of this stream of emigration was the building up of the enormous Jewish population of the Diaspora (the dispersion of the Jews) which soon outnumbered the population of Palestine. We are, of course, made constantly aware of this as we read the New Testament. Wherever Paul went on his numerous journeys through various parts of the Roman Empire he found colonies of Jews to whom he could proclaim the glad news of the Gospel. He preached in the synagogues of Ephesus, Philippi, Athens, Corinth, and many other cities, and in the capital city of Rome itself.

Strangely enough, we have no certain record that either Paul or any other missionary of the first generation ever preached in that most important center of Jewish life in the Greco-Roman world, the great Egyptian seaport and university city of Alexandria. The Jewish population was so large there that two out of the five quarters of the city were assigned to it. Here the Jews first came into significant contact with Greek life and thought, and here they first began to read the writings of pagan philosophers and poets. Out of this mingling of Greek and Jewish culture there inevitably arose a new kind of Jewish thought and practice, so different from that of Palestine that we call it Alexandrian (or Hellenistic) Judaism. Its greatest thinker was Philo Judaeus, a contemporary of Jesus. His voluminous writings, attempting to reconcile Greek speculation and Old Testament history, had great influence upon the development of theology in the early Church and are still read with interest and admiration by students of the history of philosophy.

The works of Philo are but one of the products of the literary activity that flourished so luxuriantly among the Jews in the stimulating intellectual air of Alexandria. Historically, the most important monument of the Alexandrian age is the Septuagint, the Greek translation of the Old Testament. The translation was made in response to the needs of the times. There were many Jews in Egypt who deserted their ancestral religion and became complete pagans, but there were many others, probably the majority, who continued to attend the synagogues and to read the Bible of their fathers. Of course, this became increasingly difficult, even for the most devout, since they gradually forgot how to speak and even read Hebrew and Aramaic, the languages of Palestine.

No doubt there was a continuous effort, as among modern Jews, to give the young people a smattering of the ancient tongues so they could take part in the services of the synagogue, recite the traditional prayers, and read the holy books of their religion. But we know from experience how difficult it is to make youngsters study dead languages and acquire even a moderate proficiency in them! It was no less so at that time than it is now. Inevitably, the demand arose for a version of the Bible in the language of the culture to which the people belonged and which they used in ordinary daily intercourse. Over the course of time, beginning in the third century B.C., the books of the Semitic Old Testament were translated into Greek, and thus the Septuagint took form.

The name Septuagint (from the Latin for *seventy*, hence often referred to by the symbol *LXX*) is derived from a famous, though improbable, story which the Jews told to explain how the version arose. It was said the initiative in making the translation came originally, not from the Jews, but from the Greeks. The classical form of the legend is found in an interesting ancient book called *Aristeas to Philocrates* (or *The Letter of Aristeas*). This purports to be a letter written by a certain Aristeas, a pagan official of the Egyptian court, to his brother. According to him, King Ptolemy Philadelphus, the Greek ruler of Egypt, ordered Demetrius, his royal librarian, to collect as many of the books in the world as possible. Since the Alexandrian library contained the greatest collection of books in ancient times, the story thus far is in accord with history. It then goes on to relate that Demetrius suggested the inclusion of the Jewish books of the Law, but explained that these works were written in another language and alphabet and would have to be translated before they could be used to any advantage. The king, much attracted by the prospect of adding these to his library, sent an embassy (of which Aristeas himself was a member) to Jerusalem with lavish gifts for the Temple and a formal request that seventy-two men, six from each of the tribes of Israel, be dispatched to Egypt to make an official translation of the Scriptures.

As might be expected, the high priest was greatly flattered and promptly acceded to Ptolemy's request. When the seventy-two elders arrived in Egypt, the king entertained them at a magnificent banquet during which he engaged them in philosophical conversation and was much impressed with their wisdom. At the conclusion of the festivities, they were taken to a secluded estate on an island and there began the work of translation. By strange coincidence the work was completed in exactly seventy-two days, after which it was solemnly read in the presence of the king. The story ends with an account of how the elders were sent back to Palestine, laden with honors and more tangible rewards.

Because seventy-odd men were engaged in the translation (some versions of the legend say seventy instead of seventy-two) the name Septuagint came to be attached to the work. The story told by Aristeas relates only to the translation of the Law (the first five books of the Bible), but in common parlance the name is applied to the whole Greek version of the Old Testament.

The story has been told here because of its intrinsic interest and because it accurately reflects some aspects of the general situation in Egypt in the Alexandrian age.

However, it is generally recognized to be legend and not history. The motive which gave rise to it is obvious enough. Confronted with the magnificent cultural accomplishments of the Greek world, the Jews were thrown onto the defensive and naturally became anxious to present their own national achievements in as favorable a light as possible. This was the motive that much later inspired Josephus to write the *Antiquities of the Jews* in which he attempted to show that the history of the Jewish people was as ancient as that of the Greeks and Romans and that their culture was no less worthy of honor.

The story told in *The Letter of Aristeas* is merely one of many efforts to show that the culture of the Jews inspired respect in the minds of powerful and educated pagans. For us, the principal interest of this curious little book, apart from the explanation of the name Septuagint, is the insight it gives into the position and attitudes of Jews in the Hellenistic world.

When we know what the Septuagint is, we are in a position to go one step further and define the Apocrypha: *The Apocrypha consists of those books, or parts of books, which are found in the Septuagint, but not in the Hebrew Old Testament.* A slight qualification will have to be made in a moment, but this is accurate enough for most purposes.

The Greek-speaking Jews of Alexandria had a different understanding of the canon of Scripture from that of the Jews of Palestine, and they included among their sacred books a number of works which had either been composed in Alexandria or had become popular there. Some scholars say this means that the Alexandrian Canon was larger than the Palestinian; others prefer to say simply that Alexandrian Jews drew a less definite line between canonical and noncanonical books, at least with respect to those which lay outside the Pentateuch. The distinction is largely a technical one and unimportant for our purpose. What can be stated with certainty is that the Jews of Palestine did not accept as canonical in any sense the extra books which were so popular in Alexandria.

Our English Apocrypha contains all these books plus three more of somewhat special character: II Esdras, which was never a part of the Septuagint; the Prayer of Manasses, which appears in some Septuagint manuscripts among the canticles appended to the Psalter, but seems to have had no official status; and I Esdras, which is regularly included in extant manuscripts of the Septuagint, but appears to be merely a fragment of an alternative (perhaps older) translation of the canonical books of Chronicles, Ezra, and Nehemiah, which are also present in the Septuagint in their complete form. Our original definition needs to be qualified by this latter statement, but for the moment we have a good working rule if we think of the Apocrypha as representing the difference between the Alexandrian and Palestinian canons of Scripture.

How Did Christians Come to Think of These Books as "Apocryphal"? When Christians of the first few centuries spoke of the Old Testament, they meant the Septuagint rather than the Hebrew Bible. This was natural since the New Testament was written in Greek and the Early Christian Church was a Greek-speaking Church. Of course, the situation had been different for our Lord and the original disciples, for they were Palestinian Jews who spoke Aramaic and understood Hebrew. For them the Hebrew Scriptures were the Bible. But later Christians were mostly Gentiles, who could not read the Semitic languages and for whom the Scriptures necessarily meant the Septuagint.

This explains a curious fact which all careful readers must have noticed. If one takes the trouble to look up a reference made by a New Testament writer to some passage in the Old Testament, in many cases he will find that our Old Testament (translated from the Hebrew) says something quite different. So, for example, Hebrews 10:5 contains a quotation from Psalm 40 which runs "Sacrifice and offering thou wouldest not, but *a body hast thou prepared me.*" If one looks up this verse in the King James version of the Psalter (40: 6) he will find it reads ". . . *mine ears hast thou opened.*" The same epistle relates in 11: 21 that Jacob "worshipped, leaning upon the top of his *staff,*" a reference to Genesis 47: 31. But the English Old Testament states in that passage that he "bowed himself upon the *bed's* head." In both cases the author of Hebrews is quoting from the Septuagint whereas our common English translations of the Old Testament are made directly from the Hebrew. Historically, the most serious single difference between the Septuagint and the Hebrew is with regard to the quotation of Isaiah 7: 14 made in Matthew 1: 23. Matthew reads "a *virgin* shall be with child and bring forth a son," although the original Hebrew reads "young woman," as the Revised Standard Version now reminds us. These examples are sufficient to illustrate that the Septua-

13

gint rather than the Hebrew was the authoritative Old Testament for Christians of the age in which most of the New Testament was written.[2]

The fact that the Septuagint had such great prestige among Christians soon led the Jews to react violently against it, although once they had esteemed it so highly as to believe it as inspired as the Hebrew. A later version of the Aristeas legend told that the seventy-two translators were put into different cells and each given the task of translating the whole of the Law. When they finished, it was discovered that their translations were identical down to the smallest detail, plain proof that the work had been done under the guidance of the Holy Spirit! But when the Septuagint became the Christian Bible, Jewish feelings completely changed. In arguing with Christians, Jewish apologists were constantly being confronted with proof texts which were not to be found in the Hebrew scrolls used in their synagogues. Sometimes (as in the quotation mentioned above from Isaiah), important points of doctrine seemed to hang on the difference between the Greek and Hebrew texts. As a result, the Jews went to the extreme of repudiating the Septuagint altogether, characterizing it as an imposture and a fraud of the devil. One of the later

[2] The Septuagint has a special interest for Episcopalians since the Prayer Book translation of the psalms is largely based on it rather than on the Hebrew. Where the Prayer Book version differs from the King James version in actual sense (not merely in phrasing) the difference usually goes back to the Septuagint. A familiar example is the word *alway* in Psalm 19: 14, "Let the words of my mouth . . . be *alway* acceptable." The extra word is found in the Septuagint but not in the Hebrew and therefore not in the King James Version. Many other examples could be quoted.

rabbis picturesquely expressed the prevailing view when he declared that darkness fell upon the earth for three days when the Bible was translated into Greek. So completely was the Septuagint repudiated by the Jews that even the text of it would have been lost if it had not been preserved by the Church. Of course, the Jews still needed a Greek version of the Scriptures for those of their people who could not read Hebrew, but they now set to work and made other translations which followed the Hebrew text meticulously.. These newer versions are known by the names of their translators, Aquila and Theodotion. They did not, of course, include the extra books of the Alexandrian canon.

This vehement reaction of the Jews produced no serious repercussions among Christians, at least in the West, down to the end of the fourth century. The Septuagint, or some translation of it such as the Old Latin, continued to be the official Bible of the Church. Since, in spite of the acrimonious controversy between Jews and Christians, no essential point of Christian doctrine really depended on the difference between the two versions, no great harm was done, although certain passages of Scripture were necessarily misunderstood and misinterpreted.

The person responsible for changing the attitude of the Church toward the Septuagint was St. Jerome, one of the greatest Biblical scholars who ever lived. Some have questioned his title to sanctity, at least in the modern technical sense, but none have doubted his learning. Commissioned by Pope Damasus (c. A.D. 383) to make a new and more accurate translation of the Bible into Latin, which had finally become the language of the Western Church, Jerome's exploratory studies soon revealed the deficiencies of the Septuagint and the need of making an altogether new translation from the Hebrew. He already knew something of the language, but now set to work to master it in earnest. In order to assure the accuracy of his work, he frequently consulted with Jewish rabbis, one of whom is said to have assisted him at actual peril to his own life. Since Jerome's translation, which came to be called the Vulgate (or popular version), was made under papal direction, it soon became the standard Bible of the Church in the West and remains the official Bible of the Roman Catholic Church to the present day.

But what was St. Jerome to do about the extra books, those that were in the Septuagint but not to be found in the Hebrew at all? This was a real problem. Jerome was convinced from his study of the evidence that only those books found in Hebrew (or partly in Aramaic, as in the case of Ezra and Daniel) were fully authoritative. All the other books he lumped together as of dubious, or at least secondary, value and these he called, not too appropriately, Apocrypha, meaning "books hidden away."

The name Apocrypha comes to us, therefore, directly from St. Jerome, the patron saint of Biblical scholarship. By the terms of his commission, Jerome nevertheless had to deal with these extra books in some fashion. Two of them, Tobit and Judith, he translated very hastily from Semitic manuscripts which were extant in his day. He also translated the additions to Daniel and Esther from the Greek, but the remaining books he simply left in their Old Latin form.

Strangely enough, although the Roman Catholic Church accepted Jerome's great translation, it did not accept his theory about the Old Testament canon. The official Old Testament of the Roman Church today has no separate section called the Apocrypha; its canon of Scripture is that of the Alexandrian Jews, and Jerome's apocryphal books are included at various places among the books translated from the Hebrew Old Testament. For convenience of reference, Roman Catholic scholars refer to the books outside the Hebrew canon as deuterocanonical, but the term is not meant to imply that they are of less authority. At the end of the whole Bible, the official Vulgate has a supplement containing three books which were widely read, but were either not a part of the Septuagint or had only a dubious claim to be regarded as such. (See p. 12.) These are the Prayer of Manasses and the books which the Vulgate calls Third and Fourth Esdras. (The two latter are included in our familiar English versions of the Apocrypha as First and Second Esdras.)

The Apocrypha After the Time of St. Jerome. With the great revival of Biblical studies which accompanied the Reformation there arose the necessity of reconsidering the whole problem of the Apocrypha. The reformers knew of Jerome's distinction between the books of the Hebrew canon and those of the Septuagint and adopted it for themselves. It was Martin Luther who took the decisive step of removing the apocryphal books from among the strictly canonical books and putting them into a separate section by themselves. Along with the extra books from the Latin canon the Reformed Churches naturally included the three which the Vulgate placed in the appendix. They adopted a new order for the books of the Old Testament and restored to some of them their ancient Hebrew names, so I-IV Kingdoms became I-II Samuel and I-II Kings; I-II Paralipomenon became I-II Chronicles. The books which the Septuagint, and consequently the modern Roman Catholic Bible, calls First and Second Esdras became once more, for Christians of the Reformed Churches, Ezra and Nehemiah and this made it necessary to rename the old Third and Fourth Esdras (as they are still called in Article Six of the XXXIX Articles) First and Second Esdras, a proceeding which involves endless confusion for the amateur student. In this fashion the Old Testament was reshaped according to the plan laid down nearly one thousand years before by St. Jerome, and the Apocrypha came to mean a definite part of the Scripture, printed between the Old and New Testaments.

There was a real advantage in this new arrangement since it made it easy for even the ordinary reader to see the approximate chronological relation between these books and the rest of the Old Testament. But unfortunately this new order of things also marked the beginning of a decline in the appreciation of the apocryphal books. While the reformers were well aware of the historical importance of these books, they were unanimous in refusing them any canonical recognition. This was partly the result of taking St. Jerome's theory seriously and recognizing that the Jews themselves denied their authoritative character.

These abstract considerations were undoubtedly reinforced by the fact that one of the apocryphal books, Second Maccabees, countenances the idea of the intercession of saints (15: 14) and the practice of prayers for the dead, and could even be quoted in support of the custom of offering requiem masses (12: 43-45). Since these were fundamental matters of dispute between the reformers and the old Church, it is not surprising that their attitude toward the Apocrypha sometimes tended to change from objective tolerance to active hostility. Nevertheless, the Apocrypha continued to be read and studied by Protestants and to be commonly printed as part of the Bible down to the beginning of the nineteenth century. The final blow was struck when the British and Foreign Bible Society, followed by the American Bible Society, decided in 1827 not to include the apocryphal books in their editions of the Bible. The practice swiftly spread to other publishers, for obvious reasons of economy, and it soon became difficult to obtain ordinary editions of the Bible which included them, although, as Goodspeed points out in his book, *The Story of the Apocrypha* (p. 7), they are an integral part of the King James translation and any edition which omits them is incomplete and should contain a note to that effect. The present extreme disregard for the Apocrypha has prevailed for only a little more than a hundred years, and there is strong evidence of a reaction against it. One indication of this changing point of view is the decision of the committee on the Revised Standard Version to produce a revision of the Apocrypha as well as of the Old and New Testaments.

In this, as in so many other matters, the Episcopal Church

has always taken a mediating position. On the one hand, it agrees with Protestantism in general that the apocryphal books do not have canonical authority; they are not to be used as a court of final appeal in essential matters of faith or morals. On the other hand, the Anglican Communion emphatically maintains that the Apocrypha is part of the Bible and is to be read with respect by her members. Two of the hymns used in the American Prayer Book office of Morning Prayer, the *Benedictus es* and *Benedicite*, are taken from the Apocrypha. One of the offertory sentences in Holy Communion comes from an apocryphal book (*Tob.* 4: 8-9). Lessons from the Apocrypha are regularly appointed to be read in the daily, Sunday, and special services of Morning and Evening Prayer. There are altogether 111 such lessons, many of them repeated, in the latest revised American Prayer Book Lectionary.[3] The position of the Church is best summarized in the words of Article Six of the Thirty-nine Articles: "In the name of Holy Scripture we do understand those canonical Books of the Old and New Testament, of whose authority there was never any doubt in the Church. . . . And the other Books (as Hierome [St. Jerome] saith) the Church doth read for example of life and instruction of manners; but yet doth it not apply them to establish any doctrine . . ."

Although the books of the Apocrypha are obviously to be regarded as on a somewhat lower plane than the books of the canonical Scriptures, yet the Church rates them higher than any books outside the Bible, as is shown by the fact that they alone may be read in her public worship.

[3] The books used are: II Esdras, Tobit, Wisdom, Ecclesiasticus, Baruch, Three Holy Children, and I Maccabees.

While they are not to be regarded as inspired scripture in the same sense as the books of the Old Testament proper, yet the line of demarcation is not so precise nor the difference so absolute in character as St. Jerome and the reformers thought. Without in any way surrendering our belief that the Bible is the inspired Word of God, we recognize that our ideas of inspiration today are not so mechanical as those held at certain periods in the Church's history and the limits of the canon can no longer be defined as rigidly as in the past. Few would care to defend the thesis that Ecclesiastes in the canonical Old Testament, with its essentially skeptical and hedonistic view of life, is directly inspired of God, whereas Ecclesiasticus and the Wisdom of Solomon, full as they are of fine ethical doctrine and a noble and God-centered understanding of human life, are not; or that the ferociously nationalistic book of Esther stands wholly within the stream of divine inspiration, while the gentle and deeply religious book of Tobit is completely outside. No one can seriously doubt that the canonical Old Testament as a whole is both of greater historical significance and higher religious authority than the Apocrypha, but neither can one doubt that, even though the great age of Hebrew history was past and the people of Israel were no longer stirred by the creative ferments of the prophetic age, the Holy Spirit was still moving among them. His Presence can be felt in the great passages of the Apocrypha.[4]

[4] In addition to the books of the Apocrypha, there is an extensive literature consisting of other books from the same period, such as the *Letter of Aristeas*, which never succeeded in getting into the official Septuagint. These are commonly called the Pseudepigrapha (books written under an assumed name). They are of great historical interest and some of them are referred to in the following chapters.

WHAT HAPPENED

II BETWEEN

THE TESTAMENTS

Ezra and Nehemiah. To understand the Apocrypha and the New Testament fully, it is necessary to know something of the principal events which occurred in the life of the people of Israel during the four hundred years which followed the end of Old Testament history. The Old Testament story concludes with the books of Ezra and Nehemiah. In Ezra we read of the return of the Jews from Babylon, the rebuilding of the Temple under the governorship of Zerubbabel and the pathetic attempt to pick up the threads of their old national existence. Times and conditions were against them and they were continually in danger of losing their identity, either through the violent hostility of surrounding nations, Philistines, Edomites, Ammonites and the like, or by the constant tendency of their children to intermarry with these same peoples. It was Ezra and Nehemiah who were chiefly responsible for establishing the pattern of life which enabled the Jews to keep their culture and religion intact. The pattern does not commend itself to us, since it was one of narrow and often fanatical nationalism, but it was probably the only device which could have preserved the integrity of Israel through the years which lay ahead.

The Age of Alexander the Great. Almost nothing at all is directly known of the history of the Jews during the fourth century B.C., although this period was marked by one of the most significant events in the whole story of ancient civilization—the conquest of the East by Alexander the Great. During the time of Ezra and Nehemiah, the land of the Jews was a very small province of the vast Persian Empire; shortly after 333 B.C., when Alexander defeated the army of Darius at the Battle of the Issus, Palestine became a part of the vaster Greek Empire. A brief résumé of these events is given in I Maccabees 1: 1-4. In the canonical Old Testament there is no explicit account of Alexander's career, although it is alluded to in Daniel 11: 2-3 and probably in Zechariah 9 (note especially v. 13).

For most Jews, the transfer of rule from the Persians to the Greeks could hardly have seemed anything more important than passage from oppression by one tyranny to oppression by another. Actually, it was the beginning of a new era which would profoundly and permanently affect the character of Jewish life. For one thing, the Persians had been orientals, whose type of civilization was not essentially different from that of other ancient oriental empires such as those of Assyria and Babylonia. Now, for the first time, the Jews were brought into direct contact with the civilization of the Occident and with the ways of thought and action which are basic to Western culture. Furthermore, the Greeks, in contrast to the Persians, were aggressively concerned with propagating their culture among other peoples. Alexander was not merely a conqueror. He was a missionary of Greek culture (Hellenism). Wherever he went he established Greek colonies, such as Alexandria in Egypt, which were designed to be centers of influence for the Hellenizing of the Orient. The Jews could not help but be affected by the impact of this tidal wave of new language, new ideas, and new patterns of life which was sweeping over them. The effects of the new environment in which they lived are plainly to be seen in the suave skepticism of the book of Ecclesiastes in the canonical Old Testament, which was written in the Hellenistic age, and, on the more constructive side, in the skillful appropriation of Greek philosophical terminology which marks the Wisdom of Solomon in the Apocrypha.

The danger, of course, was that the Jews would lose their religion and their identity entirely. It would be difficult to exaggerate the appeal which Greek philosophy, art, and literature had for the more intellectual and privileged members of the Jewish community. When two civilizations come in contact, it is always the tendency for the higher to absorb the lower and there can be no question that in every area but one, that of religion and morality, Greek culture was immensely superior to that of the Hebrews. From the beginning of the Greek period, there was a tendency among educated Jews to feel ashamed of the accomplishments of their own people in intellectual and

esthetic matters, and many were quite prepared to give up
all trace of Jewishness and become simply Greeks. The
author of I Maccabees speaks bitterly of these Hellenizers
who "made themselves uncircumcised, and forsook the holy
covenant, . . . and were sold to do mischief." (*I Macc.*
1: 15) Nor was this just a transient danger. It must have
existed in some way from the beginning of the period, and
we know it continued with ever-increasing force down to
the time of the great crisis which is the subject of the two
books of Maccabees. The conflict between Judaism and
Hellenism is the major theme of the period between the
Testaments. On one side were the sophisticated, material-
istic, aristocratic elements who longed for complete identi-
fication with the Hellenistic world; on the other side were
the followers of Ezra and Nehemiah, fanatical and bigoted,
sometimes ignorant and often cruel, who tended to take
an ever more uncompromising stand for the integrity of
Israel's soul. However much we may feel an emotional af-
finity for the former group, there can be no doubt that
historically it was the latter which was on the side of the
angels and, in the long run, of civilization itself.

The Jews Under the Ptolemies. When Alexander died in
Babylon at the age of thirty-three, there was no one strong
enough to take his place, so the empire quickly broke up
into several parts. This crisis is referred to explicitly in
I Maccabees 1: 5-9 and indirectly in Daniel 11: 4. Two of
these parts, the Ptolemaic and Seleucid Empires, are important in the history of the Jews and of the Apocrypha
since Palestine was ruled at different times during this

period by each of them. On Alexander's death, Egypt and its adjacent territories, including the land of Israel, fell into the hand of Ptolemy, the most able of his generals, the founder of a strong dynasty which was long to rule over that part of the world. It will be recalled that the first translation of parts of the Bible into Greek is alleged to have taken place under the second ruler of this line, Ptolemy Philadelphus (see p. 9 f). Another of Alexander's officers, Seleucus, eventually became ruler of Syria and Mesopotamia. The chief city of the Ptolemaic Empire was naturally the great new Hellenistic city of Alexandria; the capital of the Seleucids was established at Antioch in Syria, a new city Seleucus had founded for the purpose. Much of the subsequent history of the Near East is concerned with the constant rivalry between these two kingdoms, sometimes carried on by intrigue, often by prolonged and bloody warfare. The possession of Palestine, situated between the two, was one of the prime objects of contention. Daniel 11: 5-19 summarizes the history of this time, but in language which is completely intelligible only to one already familiar with the course of events.

Although Alexander's empire had broken up so swiftly and completely at his death, it must not be supposed that his program for bringing to the world the blessings of Greek culture had been frustrated. The so-called kingdoms of the Diadochi (successors), the Ptolemaic and Seleucid, as well as those with which we are not here concerned, were still devoted to the great ideal of Hellenizing the world. The various kings by the name of Seleucus and Antiochus, who ruled in Syria, like the Ptolemies in Egypt, were men of Greek descent who in varying degrees felt themselves charged to promote the use of the Greek language and the Greek way of life among their subjects. Alexandria in particular became the greatest of all centers in the ancient world for study of the arts and sciences in the Greek spirit. Here was the most famous of all libraries; here lived and worked the great mathematicians, historians, and literary critics of Hellenistic times. It is small wonder that the Jews, rapidly becoming one of the most important elements in the population of Alexandria, were dazzled by the splendor of the intellectual life around them and uncomfortably conscious of their own cultural inferiority. One can easily understand why they liked to believe that the king had arranged to include their own sacred books among the treasures of his library.

Little is known of the external history of the Jews under the rule of the Ptolemies. The whole period from the death of Alexander (323 B.C.) to 198 B.C., during most of which the land of Israel was a part of the Egyptian Empire, is almost a complete blank except for a few incidents told by Josephus and the small crumbs of fact which underlie the legends of the Aristeas document and the so-called III Maccabees (see p. 74 f). In Palestine it was a time of comparative peace. Apart from occasional battles and rumors of battles between the two kingdoms to the north and south, there was little to disturb the surface calm of a people who were chiefly engaged in the unending struggle to make a living and to transmit their spiritual heritage to their children. The greatest single accomplishment of the Palestinian Jews in this age, although we know of it only by inference, was the final editing of most of the Old Testament books and the collecting of canonical literature into a single body. Before the beginning of the Ptolemaic period, the only Bible the Jews had was the Pentateuch; at the end of it they could speak naturally of "the law, the prophets and other writings" (Prologue to Ecclesiasticus) as a well-recognized body of literature.

Under the Seleucids. Eventually, the pendulum of empire began to swing toward Syria, the other great kingdom of the Hellenistic orient. A new and vigorous monarch, Antiochus III, often called "the Great," ascended the Seleucid throne and made another, and this time successful, effort to add Palestine to his dominions. The defeat of Ptolemy V, a mere child, by the forces of Antiochus determined that the future fate of Israel should be linked with Syria rather than with Egypt. This decisive event is cryptically described in Daniel 11: 10-16 which tells how "the king of the north" (Antiochus) defeated "the king of the south" (Ptolemy) and then came to stand in Palestine, "the glorious land."

The first few years of life under Seleucid rule were as peaceful as those under the Ptolemies; the chief difference was that now taxes had to go to Antioch instead of Alexandria. Certainly, life was no more difficult for the Jews than for many other subject peoples of the Empire. If such conditions of quiet and tolerance had continued to prevail, it is entirely possible that Israel would have disappeared from among the nations. Even the rigorous system established by Ezra and Nehemiah was subject to attack by

internal decay when there were no obvious enemies to
fight against. It had been easy in the fifth century to arouse
resistance to hostile neighbors; it was much more difficult
in the second century to lead a successful battle against the
infiltration of alien ideas. The Greek language, Greek
thought, and even Greek religion were winning many
friends among the Jews and, in the long run, Hebrew faith
might have succumbed to the slow attrition of the years.
But this was not to be. A sudden crisis of unprecedented
violence aroused the nation to its peril and stirred its
sleeping energies.

A new king, Antiochus IV, came to the Seleucid throne
in the year 175 B.C. The impression he left on the people
of Israel can be gathered from the description of him in
books which come from this period: "a vile person" (*Dan.*
11: 21), "eyes like the eyes of a man and a mouth speaking
great things" (*Dan.* 7: 8), "a wicked root" (*I Macc.* 1: 10),
"the murderer and blasphemer" (*II Macc.* 9: 28). It was
customary for both the Seleucid and Ptolemaic kings to
adopt some special epithet as part of their royal title in
order to distinguish them from others of the same name;
Antiochus took the name Epiphanes, meaning "God made
manifest." The title was not remarkable in the Orient
where all kings were believed in some way to partake of
divinity, but to those who hated him, and they were many,
the name came to be a symbol of his character and ungodly
pretensions. He was a curious mixture of wise man and
fool, democrat and tyrant. At night he could wander
about the streets of Antioch with a few cronies like any
common citizen; but he also had a love of gorgeous specta-

cles and was guilty of the most ferocious cruelty when his anger was aroused.

His wrath against the Jews seems to have been inspired by a revolt which took place in Jerusalem while he was engaged in a campaign against Egypt, when Roman interference had thwarted him at the very moment of victory. A rumor reached the Jewish capital that Antiochus was dead and one of the parties which had been struggling for control of the high-priesthood seized the opportunity for open rebellion. It was enough for Antiochus to have been humiliated by the Romans; he had no intention of having his authority defied within his own dominions, so on his return from Egypt he turned aside to punish the Jews for their presumption. His soldiers massacred many of the citizens, and he himself not only robbed the treasury of the Temple but blasphemously entered the holy of holies. (*II Macc.* 5: 5-16) Now that he had lost the opportunity to conquer Egypt, he was resolved at least to make his own southern borders secure by stamping out disaffection among his Jewish subjects, and since their peculiar and fanatical religion seemed the main source of their disloyalty, he at length determined that that religion must be suppressed. He ordered all copies of the Law to be destroyed, forbade circumcision and the observance of the Sabbath, desecrated the Temple of Jehovah in Jerusalem, and set up there an altar on which swine (the most unclean of animals to the Jews) were sacrificed to the Olympian Zeus. (*I Macc.* 1: 41-63) This altar was the object which I Maccabees (1: 54) and Daniel (11: 31) call "the abomination of desolation" or "the abomination that maketh desolate." (See also

Mark 13: 14) Thus, Antiochus inaugurated the first religious persecution in the history of the world.

It is unnecessary at this point to relate subsequent developments in great detail, since the reader may discover these for himself in the two books of Maccabees in the Apocrypha. We shall here content ourselves with a brief summary.

The Maccabean Revolt. Armed resistance to the policy of Antiochus broke out in the little village of Modin in the family of an aged priest by the name of Mattathias. The old man himself precipitated the revolt by slaying both the king's officer who came to enforce the royal decree and a villager who showed himself willing to apostatize. Having given the signal for rebellion, Mattathias and his supporters fled to the hills where they began a guerilla war against the forces of the king. Shortly after this, Mattathias died and the leadership of the now popular cause fell to his five vigorous sons, first of all to Judas who was nicknamed the Maccabee, perhaps meaning the *hammer*. The war, described with great factual accuracy in I Maccabees and with considerable romantic elaboration in II Maccabees, continued for about three years, at the end of which the Jews regained possession of the major part of Jerusalem and were able to rededicate the desecrated temple. This happy event has been commemorated ever since by the festival of Hanukkah meaning Dedication; (*I Macc.* 4: 59). The feast is referred to in the New Testament (*John* 10: 22), and is observed by Jews today at about the same time as our Christmas.

Although the Temple had been purged of its heathen defilements, the Syrians had by no means given up their intention of subduing the rebellious little nation. Even when Antiochus Epiphanes died, the struggle was continued by his successors, although for the most part unsuccessfully. Judas himself was killed in one of these later battles, but his place was immediately taken by his brother Jonathan. As time went on, the character of the war changed. In the beginning it had been a fight merely for freedom to worship God, but as the latent national energies of the Jews came to be more and more deeply stirred, it became a war for political independence and even for the subjugation of neighboring peoples.

There were some among the Jews who were unhappy about this shift of emphasis, particularly the so-called Assideans (also spelled Hasideans and, in Hebrew, Chasidim). This was a party of the ultra-devout, who clung tenaciously to the religion of their fathers, but were inclined toward pacifism, because of their conviction that deliverance from the yoke of the heathen must come from God, not man. They had consented to support Judas and the rebellion because no other course seemed open, but when religious freedom was finally won and the Syrians showed a desire to effect a compromise, the Chasidim withdrew their support from the Maccabees, considering that their essential aims had been achieved. These people are commonly supposed to be the ancestors of the Pharisees of New Testament times, whose attitude toward the Romans was practically identical with that of the Chasidim toward the Syrians.

Jewish Independence; the Hasmonean Kingdom. Eventually, under the pressure of political rivalries within the Seleucid Empire itself, the successors of Antiochus Epiphanes were forced to come to terms with the Jews. Jonathan was recognized as high priest and on his death his brother Simon became not only high priest but actual civil ruler of a completely independent nation, officially recognized as such. In the year 143 B.C., says I Maccabees 13: 41, "the yoke of the heathen was taken away from Israel." For the first time in over four hundred years Judah was a sovereign nation. It would be pleasant to record that the Jews, having won this power against almost hopeless odds, made use of it in such a way as to do honor to their religion and ancient culture. Unfortunately, this was not to be. The new state was torn by corruption and internal jealousy, and lasted less than a hundred years.

Since all of the Maccabees of the first generation were now dead, the two remaining brothers having fallen in the course of the war, the succession fell upon Simon's son, John Hyrcanus. This is the last item of information recorded by I Maccabees. The parallel account in II Maccabees stops much earlier, before the death of Judas. The rest of the story comes to us principally from the pages of Josephus.

John Hyrcanus was not a bad ruler, but was a soldier rather than a religious man and devoted his energies chiefly to increasing the territory and enhancing the military prestige of his people. The most memorable event of his reign was the introduction of the policy of forcible conversion by which adjacent nations, notably the Idumeans

33

(the Jews' immediate neighbors to the south) were forced to accept Judaism at the point of the sword. It is during his term of rule (c. 134-104 B.C.) that we first hear specifically of the party of the Pharisees.

John was succeeded by his son, Aristobulus, who took the title king in addition to that of high priest and, in spite of having reigned for only a year (104-103 B.C.), left behind him a reputation for cruelty which might have shamed even an Antiochus Epiphanes. His brother, Alexander Jannaeus, who followed him, was probably no worse a man, but since he reigned for about twenty-seven years (c. 103-76 B.C.), had much more opportunity for exhibiting the thorough debasement of his character. He was despised by most of his subjects and particularly by the Pharisees, who were driven into open rebellion against him and then treated with almost inconceivable ferocity. Only one of the later Maccabees (now called Hasmoneans, after a distant ancestor) can claim our full respect. This is Queen Alexandra, who had been wife successively to Aristobulus and Alexander Jannaeus, and came to the throne on the death of the latter. She made friends with the Pharisees and ruled for nine years (c. 76-67 B.C.) in peace and prosperity.

The Beginning of Roman Rule. After the death of Alexandra the rottenness of the Hasmonean kingdom became intolerable. Her two sons, Aristobulus (II) and Hyrcanus (II), quarrelled over the succession and, when the Roman general Pompey on his triumphant march through the East came to Damascus, both of them sent embassies begging his intervention on their behalf. But the people of the land also sent an embassy to denounce both of them and to ask that neither be permitted to rule. Rome was glad enough to take the country under her protection (63 B.C.). Hyrcanus was installed as high priest, with some civil powers but under the oversight of Rome. So, after a brief interlude of independence, exciting but disillusioning, "the yoke of the heathen" settled down once more upon Jewish necks never again to be removed until modern times.

The years which followed were marked by further strife, partly encouraged by the struggle for power which was going on within the Roman Empire. The most dramatic events, related in minute detail by Josephus, were those connected with the rise of the Herodian dynasty. Herod "the Great," a semi-Jew, member of the Idumean nation which had been forcibly converted to Judaism in the time of John Hyrcanus, won his way to power by a clever use of violence, intrigue, and a tenuous connection with the Hasmonean house through his wife, Mariamne. Deficient though he was in moral character, he was a capable ruler and gave to the Jews a stable government within the framework of the Roman Empire, and a series of fine public buildings, the most notable of which was a new Temple to take the place of the rather shabby one which had been standing since the days of the return from Exile. In the last years of Herod's reign, Jesus Christ was born in Bethlehem of Judea and the gap which separates the Old Testament from the New was closed. With our bridge of history now complete, we may turn our attention to the literature produced during these colorful times.

III

ADDITIONS TO CANONICAL BOOKS: *DANIEL, EZRA (1 ESDRAS), AND ESTHER*

Additional Material in the Greek. While most of the apocryphal books are complete in themselves and quite independent of anything in the Hebrew Old Testament, a few of them are merely expansions of familiar Old Testament books. To put it another way, there are several books in the Septuagint which are longer than the corresponding books in the Hebrew, and the material in the Apocrypha consists of the portions found only in Greek. These are: The History of Susanna, The Song of the Three Holy Children, Bel and the Dragon, and The Rest of Esther. They are merely fragments, and in one case, that of the portions of Esther, the fragments make no sense unless they are read in conjunction with the Old Testament book to which they belong. To these we must add I Esdras because, although in form it is a complete book, it is really an alternative version of the canonical book of Ezra and part of Nehemiah, prefaced by a brief section from Chronicles and containing a number of omissions and variations and one important addition.

Susanna. The History of Susanna, which in present editions of the Greek Bible is prefixed to Daniel and is included in the Vulgate as chapter 13 of the same book, is a little gem of a short story and probably the best known of the narratives of the Apocrypha. Like the rest of Daniel, its setting is in Babylon during the days of the Exile. It tells how Susanna, a devout and beautiful matron of the Jews, aroused the lustful passions of two elders who frequently presided over the law court which met at the house of her husband, Joacim (Joakim).

At first, they concealed their feelings even from each other. But one day, having just parted at Joacim's doorstep, ostensibly to return home for dinner, each met the other creeping back to spy on Susanna. Their embarrassment forced each of them to confess shamefacedly why he was there. The next step was to concoct a plot by which they might overcome Susanna's virtue. One day, while she was bathing, they hid themselves in the garden and, when her maids had left, rushed out and threatened to bring against her a public charge of adultery. If she did not submit to them, they were prepared to swear under oath they had caught her in the arms of a young man in that very garden. The pious Susanna refused and on the morrow was hailed before the court of Israel to be tried. Because she had no defense other than her own protestations of innocence, and the two elders were agreed in presenting their perjured testimony, she was condemned to die.

Just as Susanna was being led away to execution, the proceedings were dramatically interrupted by the shout of a young man, Daniel, who demanded the right to interrogate the witnesses. The privilege was granted him and he examined them separately as to the details of their charge against her. Specifically, he insisted upon knowing under what kind of tree the alleged crime was committed. The first elder said, "a mastick tree." Daniel's reply was in the form of an ironic pun which Goodspeed paraphrases in English by "God shall masticate *you!*" The second said "a holm tree" and Daniel answered him too with a pun, impossible to reproduce in English. Since it was evident that both were lying, Susanna was declared innocent, the two elders were executed in her stead, and Daniel became a man of great renown among the people.

The story is obviously fiction, not history, and has no connection with the book of Daniel except the name of its hero. Originally the "young youth" was undoubtedly anonymous and was identified with Daniel only when the story was introduced into the book which bears his name. Many scholars are inclined to believe that in spite of the Greek puns the story in its present form is a translation from the Hebrew. Although such a pleasant tale of virtue triumphant and evil punished hardly seems to require any special motive to account for its telling, some scholars have felt it must have a practical point. They believe it was intended to reinforce a legal reform, instituted by the Pharisees early in the first century B.C., which imposed on the courts new and more rigorous standards for the examination of witnesses. This view is possible, but it cannot be proved; if true it would give us the approximate date for the composition of the story in its present form.

The story of Susanna has always been a popular one and has frequently provided inspiration for painters. The latest to attempt the subject was Thomas Hart Benton, who effectively transferred the locale to America in the twentieth century. Without some knowledge of this book, one could hardly understand the familiar allusion in *The Merchant of Venice* where Shylock addresses Portia as "a Daniel come to judgment." It is only in the Susanna legend that Daniel appears in a legal role.

The Three Holy Children. The Song of the Three Holy Children is an integral part of the book of Daniel in the Septuagint, where it is inserted between vss. 24 and 25 of chapter 3 in the story of the three young men thrown into the fiery furnace for their obstinate refusal to worship Nebuchadnezzar's image. It consists of three parts: the prayer of Azarias (1-22), a brief narrative section which describes how the angel of the Lord reduced the terrible flame of fire to "a moist whistling wind" (23-27), and the long hymn of thanksgiving that the youths sang to celebrate their deliverance. It is evident that neither the prayer nor the hymn was originally composed for this use, since neither contains anything distinctly appropriate to the unique situation of the three young men, except v. 66 which is probably a later addition.

The prayer of Azarias is a fine example of Jewish liturgical devotion. It is chiefly concerned with Israel in the unhappy days during and immediately after the Babylonian exile: the author acknowledges Israel's guilt and prays for deliverance.

The great hymns which give this little book its title are of special interest to Episcopalians because of their use in the Prayer Book. The second part, the *Benedicite* (35-65), has been used since antiquity as one of the canticles of the Church. In the First Prayer Book (1549), it was prescribed to be said in place of the *Te Deum* during Lent, and this custom is still followed in many places. Unfortunately, there are some in the Church who never hear it at all; its excessive length, by modern standards, discourages many choirs from ever singing it. It will not seem quite so long if one realizes that it is composed somewhat in the style of the Litany with an invariable congregational response to each of the summons to praise. In this respect it is like Psalm 136, although in general literary structure it seems to have been inspired by Psalm 148. The conception of the hymn is one of overwhelming grandeur; the whole physical universe is summoned, choir by choir, to join in the praises of the Lord. The poet addresses first of all the heavens and all the celestial bodies (35-51); then the earth and everything that lives and moves upon it (52-59); finally, man himself is called upon to join creation's great symphony of praise (60-65). The concluding verses seem to have been added when the psalm was adapted to its present use. In the 1928 revision of the American Prayer Book, the opening section of the hymn (vss. 29-34) was included in Morning Prayer under the name of *Benedictus es* as a briefer alternative to the *Te Deum* and *Benedicite*.

Bel and the Dragon. In the Septuagint, two separate stories, Bel and the Dragon, follow upon the book of Daniel (and constitute chapter 14 in the Vulgate). In them, we have interesting examples of Jewish propaganda against the worship of idols. Ever since the Babylonian Exile, paganism had had great attraction for many Jews, largely because the victories of heathen nations over Israel seemed clear proof that pagan gods had superior power. In this situation, Jewish religious leaders developed an effective satirical polemic. How, they asked, could any intelligent person think of worshiping these impotent creatures, obviously made by men's hands from wood and stone? Second Isaiah (the unknown author of Isaiah 40-55) was the first to use this line of attack. Isaiah 44: 9-20 is a good example of his work. As we have noted in a previous chapter, paganism in the days of Greek rule had even greater appeal for the Jews than it had had under the Babylonians or Persians, because it represented cultural as well as military supremacy. So it is not surprising that the polemic of ridicule was still necessary. The little book called The Epistle of Jeremy (to be discussed later) is one example of this type of writing. The two short-short stories of Bel and the Dragon are intended to show the folly of paganism in all ages and in all forms, although, like the rest of the book of Daniel, their specific setting is that of the Exile.

Miss Dorothy Sayers in her *Omnibus of Crime* puts the stories of Susanna and Bel at the head of the list as the first detective stories ever written. In the Bel story, Daniel refuses to worship the chief god of Babylon (whose name is another form of the Old Testament Baal) and tells Cyrus, the Persian king, who has just become the Babylonian ruler, that he will not do honor to a lifeless image, but only to the true God of heaven and earth. When the king attempts to refute Daniel's thesis that the god is impotent by describing how much food Bel consumes every day, the latter smiles and agrees to a test of the facts. The food is to be placed in Bel's chambers and the doors sealed. If, when the room is opened the next day, the food is gone, then Daniel will have been proved an impious blasphemer and suffer the penalty of death. But, unknown to king or priests, Daniel ordered the floor of the room covered with ashes, so when the doors are opened in the morning and the king triumphantly announces that the food is gone, Daniel points laughingly to the prints of many feet which clearly show that the priests and their families had entered by a secret door and consumed the rations set out for Bel. Thereupon, says the story, the king had the priests executed and allowed Daniel to destroy Bel and his temple.

The other story, that of the dragon, is much inferior to the one just related. It states, with little semblance of historical probability, that the Babylonians worshiped a great dragon (or, better, serpent) whom Daniel destroyed by feeding an explosive mixture of pitch, fat, and hair. Enraged at this, the Babylonians cast him into a den of hungry lions for six days. There he was fed by the prophet Habakkuk, whom an angel carried by the hair of his head from Palestine to Babylon for the purpose. Daniel was eventually released unharmed from the lions' den and his adversaries were cast into it, where they were instantly devoured. Plainly, this is a second-rate version of the canonical story of Daniel in the lions' den. Preposterous as the story sounds to us, savoring more of the *Arabian Nights* than of the Bible, it undoubtedly was crudely effective among the people for whom it was designed. It dramatized for them the conflict between the impotent gods of the Greeks and the almighty God of Israel and helped them to dissolve the pretensions of paganism in hearty gusts of laughter.

I Esdras. The next of the books to be considered in this section is of less interest to the general reader, although it is a source of perennial concern to the scholar. Its very nature and origin are something of a mystery. From a purely descriptive standpoint, one can say that I Esdras is a Greek version of the Old Testament book of Ezra, partly rearranged, with about two chapters of II Chronicles prefixed (*I Esd.* 1 = *II Chron.* 35: 1—36: 21) and a brief section from the book of Nehemiah added at the end (*I Esd.* 9: 37-55 = *Neh.* 7: 73—8: 13a). In addition to this there is the long and interesting story of the Three Guardsmen (*I Esd.* 3: 1—5: 6) interpolated just before the opening words of chapter 2 in the canonical Ezra. The account of the letter to Artaxerxes which in Ezra appears in chapter 4 actually precedes the interpolated material in I Esdras (*Ezra* 4: 7-24 = *I Esd.* 2: 16-30).

The peculiarities of the book become even more remarkable and mysterious when one realizes that the Septuagint has a perfectly straightforward translation of Chronicles, Ezra, and Nehemiah, under the names of I-II Paralipomenon and Esdras (designated as Esdras B). So our apocryphal I Esdras (sometimes simply called the Greek

THE APOCRYPHA, BRIDGE OF THE TESTAMENTS

Esdras because of its difference from the Hebrew and to avoid the confusion in the numbering of the various Esdras books) seems hardly to have any excuse for existing! I Esdras is one òf the three books in the Apocrypha (I-II Esdras and the Prayer of Manasses) which is not included among the canonical books of the Vulgate but is placed in an Appendix to the New Testament (see p. 17). As we have previously noted, the Vulgate uses the names I and II Esdras for the canonical Ezra and Nehemiah, and calls our book Third Esdras (as do the Thirty-nine Articles). Here truly is a pathetic orphan among books! Its history is a problem. Its nature is obscure. And even its name is uncertain.

How did such a book ever come to be written, and why should it have been preserved? No certain answer can be given although many have been attempted. In order to get a hint of the correct solution to the puzzle, one must first realize that the four books we call I and II Chronicles, Ezra, and Nehemiah are in reality only one book. Or, to put it another way, they are the four volumes of a single work which purports to give a history of Judaism from the time of Adam to approximately the author's own day.[1] It is one of the latest books in the Old Testament. One theory assumes that it appeared in two different editions; perhaps an original edition was later revised by the writer himself. According to this theory, *both* of the editions were translated into Greek. If so, then we may regard our canonical Chronicles, Ezra, and Nehemiah, together with the transla-

[1] Robert C. Dentan, *The Holy Scriptures—A Survey* (New York: The Seabury Press), p. 70.

44

tion of them in the Septuagint, as representing one form of the book, while I Esdras would appear to be a fragment of the other, and probably older, edition. This is a mere hypothesis, but it is hard to think of a more plausible one.

A truly difficult problem is why only this fragment remains. Torrey has an ingenious explanation which is worth noting, if only for want of a better. He supposes that our I Esdras is a surviving fragment of the original Septuagint version of Chronicles-Ezra-Nehemiah. After this had been supplanted by a newer and more authoritative translation, based on the latest edition of the work, someone thought it worth while to preserve a part of the older version because of its interesting variants and especially because of the fine story of the Three Guardsmen which was no longer included in the text of the definitive edition. So he simply ripped out the middle section of his book, the part containing the material which interested him, and threw the rest away. He was careful to include a little of Chronicles and a little of Nehemiah, to show that his fragment was part of what had once been a complete work, but he was indifferent as to just where it began and ended. If this theory is correct, I Esdras is not only deficient with respect to name and form, but is not even a book; it is only a damaged excerpt, preserved almost by chance.

The ordinary reader, approaching I Esdras in the Apocrypha for the first time, will probably not care to read the whole work or to worry over the innumerable historical problems which arise when one compares it with the canonical books of Ezra and Nehemiah or with the known facts of Persian history. But he will certainly not want to miss the famous story of the Three Guardsmen (3: 1-5: 6), which is probably the one reason the book continued in circulation. The tale is not integral to the book as a whole and is probably of pagan origin. Its inclusion in the Chronicler's history was accomplished by identifying the hero with Zerubbabel, the famous builder of the second Temple (*I Esd.* 4: 13).

The plot concerns three soldiers who were on guard one night at the court of Darius, king of Persia. As they while away the monotonous hours, one of them proposes a contest of wits on the subject: "What is the strongest thing in the world?" They arrange (somewhat presumptuously, it may seem to the reader) that the sleeping king shall hear their arguments when he awakes and present the victor with a magnificent gift. Each one writes down his opinion and these are placed under the king's pillow. The first one wrote "Wine"; the second, "the King"; and the third, "Women." But the third took what appears to be an unfair advantage by adding yet a fourth word, "Truth." This awkward addition, which is the point of the whole story as it now stands, was probably made when the original pagan story was adapted to Jewish use. No Jew would acknowledge that wine, king, or woman could be the strongest thing in the world. For him, there could be nothing stronger than the eternal truth of God.

On awaking, the king readily acceded to the plan and each of the contestants presented his arguments before him in the form of a long and ingenious speech. As we should expect, the decision was in favor of the one who not only defended the superior power of women, but asserted that "above all things Truth beareth away the victory" (3: 12, and 4: 35, 41). According to the story, this third contestant was Zerubbabel who received as his prize the king's permission to rebuild Jerusalem.

The improbabilities of the story must not divert attention from the noble doctrine which it teaches: *Magna est veritas et praevalet* (Vulgate of 4:41; "great is Truth and mighty above all things," in the King James Version). This is the one great text of I Esdras, but it has been a favorite down the ages and almost by itself justifies the preservation of this curious book. While the saying has its roots in the deep moral seriousness of the ancient Hebrew mind, the thought in this particular form can hardly have been expressed by anyone except a Jew of the Hellenistic age. It is a milestone on the road which leads from the world of Old Testament thought to One who is reported to have said: "Ye shall know the truth and the truth shall make you free," and also "*I* am the way, the truth and the life."

Esther. Of less interest than the variants in the books of Daniel and Ezra are the additions to Esther. Unlike the stories of Bel and Susanna and the Three Guardsmen, this material contains nothing which is of much intrinsic value and, indeed, makes no sense unless read in the context of the canonical book. The Greek version of Esther has a very different character from the Hebrew and the chief interest which attaches to these fragments lies in seeing what that character is. The Hebrew original is a notoriously secular book that makes no mention of the name of God from beginning to end. By contrast, in the Greek version, Esther becomes a devoutly religious document. The whole plot of the story, it says, had been revealed to Mordecai (Mardocheus in Greek) by a vision from God (11: 2—12 and 10: 5-13); both Mordecai and Esther are represented as reciting lengthy and conventional prayers when the great crisis arose (13: 8—14: 19); Esther is made to palliate the scandal of her service in the court of a heathen king by explaining how distasteful it had been to her (14: 15-18); and the king's change of mind when Esther dared to come into his presence is attributed to God's direct intervention (15: 8). Also, in order to give greater verisimilitude to the story, the alleged texts of two letters have been included in it (13: 1-7 and chap. 16).

In reading the apocryphal sections, it is important to observe that in their present form they are not in proper order. The following guide will assist the reader in understanding their relationship to the story: The book in its Greek shape begins with Mordecai's dream, etc. (11: 2—12: 6). Then follows canonical Esther 1: 1—3: 13. At this point, apocryphal Esther purports to give the text of the letter in which the king ordered the destruction of the Jews (13: 1-7). Between chapters 4 and 5 of canonical Esther are inserted the prayers of apocryphal Esther 13: 8—14: 19. Apocryphal Esther 15: 1-16 is an expanded version of canonical Esther 5: 1-2. After canonical Esther 8: 13, which tells of another letter of the king, the apocryphal book again inserts what is supposedly the actual text of the letter (chapter 16). Finally, at the end of the whole story in the canonical book, the reader must turn back to the beginning of apocryphal Esther and read 10: 4—11: 1. The reason for this illogical arrangement, in which the last item actually appears first, is that our apocryphal version is taken from the Latin Vulgate. Jerome first translated the Hebrew book as it stands and then immediately (and logically) added to it the conclusion of the Greek book. Only then did he go back to translate the other sections which are peculiar to the Greek.

The two versions of Esther are interesting examples of two different types of Judaism: one the nationalistic type represented by the canonical book; the other a thoroughly religious kind. The division of opinion among the Jews as to whether they are primarily a nation or a religion has persisted down to the present time and is a source of frequent controversy in contemporary Jewish circles. The issue was very much alive in New Testament times, and our Lord certainly had to take His stand with regard to it. While the Gospels do not reveal that He ever concerned Himself with this particular book (and it is hard to believe the book of Esther in any form would have had much appeal for Him), there can be little doubt that the apocryphal book, with its strong sense of God's overruling Providence, would have been more congenial to His mind than the story in its familiar canonical form. Which of the two forms of the book is the older is still something of an open question, although it seems more likely that the Greek is a devout expansion of the Hebrew rather than that the Hebrew is a secularizing abridgment of an older edition now found only in the Greek.

IV

TWO ROMANTIC TALES:
TOBIT AND JUDITH

Tobit. For many readers, the book of Tobit is the crown of the Apocrypha. It is a colorful oriental tale, much in the style of the *Arabian Nights*, and contains all the elements which make a story appealing in any age: exotic setting, love interest, travel, dangerous adventure, conflict with superhuman evil, and, withal, a happy ending! But while it is obviously fiction, and good fiction, the Christian reader will be especially interested in reading it for the picture it gives of Jewish piety at its simplest and best. The theology of the book and its ethical standards are not those of the Hebrew Old Testament but of later Judaism, the Judaism in which our Lord grew up and in the midst of which He ministered. If we wish to view from within, and sympathetically, the life of Jews in New Testament times, such people as Mary and Joseph, Elizabeth and Zacharias, Anna and Simeon, and the twelve apostles, there is no better place to do it than in the book of Tobit. Certainly there is none more accessible to the average reader.

The scene of the story is ancient Assyria among the Jews who had been taken captive when the Northern Kingdom was destroyed and the ten tribes carried into exile. Its hero, Tobit, is pictured as a respected member of the exiled community, full of kindness and good works, and particularly famed for his courage in providing decent burials for the bodies of fellow countrymen slain by the Assyrians. While burying one of them, Tobit lost his eyesight through a curious accident and could not be healed by the physicians. He prayed that he might die rather than continue to live in so miserable a state.

At this point (*Tobit* 3: 7) the scene shifts and another though related plot is introduced. The reader's attention is directed to the city of Ecbatane (more correctly Ecbatana), in the distant kingdom of Media. Tobit, long before (1: 14), had deposited with a friend in Rages, another Median city, the sum of ten talents (c. $20,000), a fact which becomes important in the later development of the story. At Ecbatana we are introduced to Sara, an unhappy girl who had been married seven times; each of her husbands had died before the marriage could be consummated. Sara's husbands had not died by accident, but were murdered by a foul demon, Asmodeus, who had fallen in love with her. Like Tobit, Sara despaired of her life and prayed that God might take it from her. Sara and Tobit happened to say their prayers at the same time and both were heard by God, who sent the angel Raphael (meaning "God heals") to answer them (chap. 3).

Tobit did not know, of course, that his prayer had been favorably heard, but he now remembered the large sum of money he had left on deposit in Media and desired, before he died, to see it safely in the hands of his beloved son, Tobias. Summoning Tobias, he prepared him for the long journey and gave him fatherly counsel as to his manner of life. This fine ethical section (chap. 4) is worth the reader's special attention. It is particularly notable for its emphasis on almsgiving, the most important act of piety for Jews of New Testament times and one concerning which Jesus had a good deal to say (e. g. *Matt.* 6: 2-4). Here also is to be found, in negative form, the "Golden Rule" (vs. 15), evidence of how close our Lord's teaching was to the best in the Judaism of His day, although He always seemed to go at least one step beyond it.

Tobias secured as a servant and guide, to accompany him on his journey, a stranger who called himself Azarias, but who was actually the angel Raphael in disguise (chap. 5). An unusual and touching note in the narrative is the observation that Tobias's dog also went with him (5: 16). This is particularly remarkable in that the dog was ordinarily regarded as an unclean animal. (The dog Toby in the traditional Punch and Judy show is said to derive his name from this story.) The first night of their journey, they camped by the river Tigris where Tobias was attacked by a man-eating fish. Instructed by his companion, Tobias seized the fish and removed the heart, the liver, and the gall. He is told that the heart and liver are effective when burned for driving out demons and that the gall is a powerful medicine for his father's peculiar type of blindness.

As they approached the city where Sara dwelt, the angel disclosed to Tobias that she was his predestined bride. As her kinsman, he alone had the right to take her. Tobias was inclined to demur at the privilege offered him since he had heard the fate of her seven previous husbands, but Raphael (Azarias) tells him how to burn the heart and liver of the fish with incense in the bridal chamber and thus drive away the demon forever (chap. 6).

They were welcomed with open arms in the home of Sara's parents, and Tobias lost no time in making his proposal of marriage. Raguel, her father, conscientiously explained what had happened to her previous husbands, but Tobias insisted on the immediate completion of the marriage ceremony (chap. 7). The father was so uncertain of the outcome that he dug a grave for Tobias on the wedding night, but the fortunate bridegroom followed exactly the instructions of his angelic companion, and the demon was routed and fled to upper Egypt where the angel caught and bound him. Tobias and Sara offered a brief but beautiful prayer as the wedding night began (8: 5-8). In the morning, when Raguel discovered that his fears had not been realized, he blessed God for His mercy and ordered the newly dug grave to be filled. Afterward, Tobias sent Raphael to collect the money due him from his kinsman in Rages and settled down for the fortnight's wedding feast which his father-in-law prescribed (chap. 9).

Meanwhile, the scene shifts back to Nineveh (10), where we see Tobit and his wife anxiously awaiting their son's return, wondering if evil had befallen him. The reader, of course, knows the happy outcome of the journey and is permitted to anticipate the happiness which will soon be theirs. At Raphael's suggestion, he and Tobias reached home before the bride and, after the greetings were over, Tobias administered the cure for his father's blindness. So Tobit was able to go out himself and meet his new daughter-in-law at the gate of the city. The joyful reunion was followed by another wedding feast, of seven days' duration (chap. 11). When Tobit and Tobias attempted to settle the wages of Azarias, to whom their present happiness was chiefly due, he revealed that he was not a mortal servant, but the angel Raphael—one of the seven who present men's prayers before the throne of God. Raphael confesses he had been with them only in the form of a vision and had neither drunk nor eaten anything in all that time. All that he had done, he says, had been commissioned of God in answer to their prayers. Included in his discourse is some further ethical instruction, with the usual emphasis upon almsgiving (12: 6-10). After Raphael's ascent to heaven, the book concludes with a psalm of thanksgiving composed by Tobit and an account of Tobit's death and his son's return to live in Ecbatana where, before he died, he heard of the fall of the wicked city of Nineveh.

The air of simple goodness and heartfelt piety which pervades the book provides a sufficient clue to the purpose for which it was written. There is no reason to suppose that the author had any purpose beyond that of entertaining his readers and at the same time holding up for their imitation an example of a human life filled with love toward men and prayerful submission toward God. No doubt, many of those who first heard the beatitudes of Jesus were people just like this—poor in spirit, merciful, hungering and thirsting after righteousness. These were the people among whom the Gospel message most readily found a hearing. As to the book itself, it was undoubtedly written originally in either Hebrew or Aramaic—although only the Greek translation has survived—and probably in the neighborhood of Jerusalem. Its most likely date is late in the third century B.C., in the quiet days before the Maccabean persecutions had brought so much bitterness into Jewish life. The author, of course, is unknown. Of special interest to the student of the history of theology is the book's emphasis upon what we today would call "personal religion." It is filled with a profound sense of God's direct concern for the welfare of His children and of the value of prayer, fasting, and almsgiving as chief activities of the devout life (12: 8). The reader will remember that these are just the practices our Lord singles out for special discussion in the Sermon on the Mount (*Matt.* 6: 1-18). Tobit is especially interesting for its elaborate doctrine about angels (and demons), something unparalleled in the Old Testament except for the book of Daniel (which is later than Tobit), but quite familiar to us from the New Testament.

Judith. The second of the two romantic tales, the book of Judith, which is the subject of this section, has just as good a story as that of Tobit and a more plausible one, but for Christian readers it is far less appealing. It relates the daring exploit of a heroic woman who used her remarkable endowments of beauty and personal charm to rescue her people from disaster in time of war. The closest parallel to the theme is found in the book of Esther, but the plots are entirely different; and Judith is morally superior to Esther (at least to the canonical Esther) in that the moving power behind the heroine's brave deed is represented as religious rather than purely nationalistic.

Like Tobit, the story of Judith is sheer fiction. The author makes this clear by giving his heroine an ideal name (Judith means Jewess) and by setting the story in "the reign of Nabuchodonosor (Nebuchadnezzar), who reigned in Nineve" (1: 1), over the Assyrians in the days immediately after the return of the Jews from captivity (4: 3). This is like putting a modern story "in the days of Woodrow Wilson who was president of the Confederate States of America shortly after the end of World War II." Such confusion can hardly be other than deliberate and is perhaps intended to warn the reader against taking the story as literal history.

The opening chapters (1-7) merely set the stage for the adventure which is to follow. They tell us how, when Nebuchadnezzar had gone to war against the Medes, the people of the West, including Syria and Palestine, had refused to come to his assistance (chap. 1). After the war was won, he resolved to punish the nations who had flouted his request and sent Holofernes, the general of his armies, to subdue them. Everywhere Holofernes met with great success and forced the subjugated peoples to worship Nebuchadnezzar in place of their own gods, until at last he came to the borders of Judea (chaps. 2-3). Having heard of his triumphant progress through the neighboring countries, the Jews were terrified and began making frantic preparations to resist him, preparations which involved prayer and fasting as well as the mobilization of their forces.

The concern of the story now narrows down to the city of Bethulia (unknown otherwise, but perhaps a fictitious name for Shechem), near which Holofernes had encamped. In getting ready for the attack, the general consulted with men of neighboring countries who were familiar with the geography of the land and the character of its inhabitants. One of the representatives, Achior, an Ammonite, asserted that the Jews were invincible so long as they were faithful to the law of their God (5: 5, 20-21). Holofernes could hardly be expected to credit such a report, and not only denounced Achior for the implied insult to the power of Nebuchadnezzar, but ordered him to be bound and handed over to the Jews (6: 1-2, 10-13). When the men of Bethulia discovered him lying in the no-man's land between the city and the enemy camp, they brought him in, treated him kindly, and learned what had gone on in the council of war (6: 14ff). In the meantime, Holofernes decided to follow the good advice of some of the other surrounding peoples who were now allied with him and not attempt to storm the fortifications of the Jews. It seemed easier and more likely of success simply to lay siege to the city and try to starve it out. After thirty-four days, the water supply of Bethulia was almost entirely exhausted and the people began to accuse the leaders of being responsible for their plight and to urge immediate capitulation. Ozias, one of the elders, begged them to hold out for five more days and promised to surrender if help did not arrive by then (chap. 7).

The events leading up to the crisis having been fully described, the stage is set for the appearance of the heroine. She is introduced at the beginning of chapter 8, a widow for more than three years, remarkable for both her piety and her beauty. Upon hearing of the plan to surrender at the end of a stated period, she delivered an indignant speech to the elders of the city in which she reproached them for attempting to force God's hand. "God is not as man, that he may be threatened," she says (8: 16). One must patiently wait for Him to act in His own good time. The elders sincerely apologized for their error and added that only a great extremity could have driven them to it. Judith then announced she had a plan of her own to defeat the enemy, although she refused to disclose its precise nature. Chapter 9 is taken up entirely with the prayer spoken by Judith before she sets out on her perilous adventure. In it she begs that God will prosper the deceit she is about to practice. Her prayer finished, she removed her widow's garments and beautified herself with all the aids which wealth and cosmetics could provide. Then, with her maid and in the sight of all the people, she headed out through the city gate straight toward the camp of the enemy. There she introduced herself to the sentries as a Hebrew woman who was fleeing the imminent fall of the city and desired to show the Assyrians an easy way to bring about its collapse, promptly and without casualties (10: 1-13).

Holofernes received her graciously in all the splendor of his tent and encouraged her to tell her story. She confirmed the report which Achior had already given of the

Jews. It was true that they could not be defeated unless they had sinned; but now they were going to sin and their doom was sure, for in the extremity of the famine they were about to violate God's law by eating forbidden animals and the offerings which were intended for God alone (10: 14—11: 23). Holofernes offered her refreshment at his own table, but she refused on religious grounds and asked the privilege of eating only the food she had brought in her bag. About midnight she asked permission of the general to go out of the camp through the sentry lines to bathe at a nearby spring and to say her prayers. Suspecting nothing, Holofernes ordered the guards to give free passage to Judith and her maid (12: 1-9). For three nights she did this. At last the opportunity came for which she had been waiting. Holofernes was determined to enjoy this beautiful Jewish woman to the full and arranged a magnificent banquet for her in his tent. Once again she showed her piety by refusing to eat the delicacies provided, but nevertheless joined in the festivities and ate the food which her maid had brought. At last the general, now almost stupefied with wine, dismissed all his servants and Judith found herself alone with him. All her plans had been directed toward this moment, so without hesitation she invoked the God of her people and, taking Holofernes' sword in one hand and his hair in the other, severed the head from his body. Now all that remained to be done was to put the head in the bag she had brought and to march out, as on the previous nights, into the darkness beyond the borders of the camp.

Without difficulty she and her maid returned to Bethulia

where she displayed her bloody trophy and called on all the people to praise God for the great deliverance He had accomplished by her hand (chap. 13). In the morning they hung the head of Holofernes on the wall of the city and all their warriors rushed out boldly to attack the Assyrian encampment. As soon as the guards saw the approaching army, they ran to the general's tent to arouse him to the defense, but found nothing but his headless body (chap. 14). Ungovernable panic struck the Assyrian host and all the Jews had to do was to pursue them and despoil their camp (chap. 15). The book concludes with a psalm composed by Judith to celebrate her victory, together with a brief account of her later years, and her death at the age of 105.

There are many things in this grim story which are shocking to the refined sensibilities of Christians—the apparent delight in bloodshed, the treacherous conduct which is the principal theme of the story, and the excessive concern with observance of dietary laws as the chief evidence of piety. These characteristics cannot be denied, and because of them the story has none of the immediate appeal of Tobit. Nevertheless, it would be an error to overlook the positive qualities of the book. The virtues it holds up for imitation are not gentleness and kindliness, as in the case of Tobit, but rather courage, steadfast devotion to a cause, and genuine concern for religion, limited as that religion may appear to the modern reader. The one quality it has in common with Tobit is a pervading belief in the importance and efficacy of prayer. The most unforgettable scene in the story is when Judith pauses, sword in hand, just before the fatal stroke, to ask God's help: "Strengthen me, O Lord God of Israel, this day (13: 7)."

If we find the close connection of bloodshed and faith in God somewhat shocking today, it is of course partly because most of us have no personal experience of war or persecution and have never known the intensity of feeling which may move the population of a city undergoing siege. When Christian people in modern times find themselves in similar desperate circumstances, their emotions do not seem to be particularly different. To say this is in no way to justify either their attitude or the narrow and bellicose spirit of the book of Judith, but it may help us to feel a human kinship with its heroine and give us some appreciation of the sturdy virtues the book commends.

Judith seems to have been written originally in Hebrew and probably in Palestine, although, as in the case of Tobit, only the Greek translation made in Alexandria remains. The militancy of its spirit certainly suggests a date after the Maccabean revolt, perhaps shortly after the middle of the second century B.C. "Nebuchadnezzar," who sets himself up as sole God and proposes to destroy the religion of the Jews as well as their nation, clearly reflects the character of Antiochus Epiphanes. The story is one which has captured the imagination of many generations of readers and has frequently provided a subject for poets and artists. Incidents from the story have been illustrated by Botticelli and Tintoretto and a famous statue by Donatello commemorates its heroine.

TWO VALUABLE BOOKS

V | OF HISTORY:

I AND II MACCABEES

I Maccabees. If accuracy is the chief test for judging a book of history, I Maccabees would rate very high. It is a sober, straight-forward account of the events connected with the Maccabean revolt and the establishment of the second Jewish Kingdom. While the author is obviously a partisan of the Maccabees and tells his story in order to preserve the memory of their great deeds, yet he is content to let the story carry its own message without any imaginative heightening of the facts. It is the best piece of historical writing in the Old Testament after the "court history" of David (*II Sam.* 9-20), written nearly a thousand years before. We shall see that history can be told in quite different fashion when we come to examine II Maccabees later in this chapter.

Like many other books of the Apocrypha, I Maccabees was written originally in Hebrew, probably in Palestine, although only the Greek translation has survived. Its author is entirely unknown, but he certainly deserves high rank among the historians of the ancient world. He was obviously a man of conservative religious temper, on the whole a precursor of the Sadducees rather than the Pharisees. This, in part, explains the excellence of his history, for the traditional cast of his mind forbade him to indulge in fantasies based on any belief in angels, spirits, or demons. He describes no miracles, no striking supernatural interventions, and makes no reference to the doctrine of the resurrection of the dead—an important theme in II Maccabees and Daniel. This lack of supernatural coloring, it is true, gives a somewhat prosaic complexion to the narrative. It is not so exciting a book as II Maccabees, but this is surely a small price to pay for so remarkable an example of objective historical writing. If the reader sometimes feels oppressed by the unadorned sobriety of the tale, as well as by the bewildering complexity of events and the apparent superfluity of proper names, he should pause to pay homage to a writer, who, amid the emotional tensions of his age, can set down so accurate a record of one of the great crises of the human spirit.

The period covered by the book (c. 168-136 B.C.) is from the outbreak of the Maccabean revolt to the death of Simon, the last of the five sons of Mattathias. The plan of the book becomes clear when we see that each portion of it deals with a particular member of the family of the Maccabees. Chapter 1 briefly describes the background of the conflict; in chapter 2 we are told the story of Mattathias; the exploits of Judas are the theme of 3: 1—9: 22; Jonathan is the hero of 9: 23—12: 53; and the account of Simon's career then occupies the rest of the book.

The forward movement of the drama can be seen if one will keep in mind the following brief outline: When the story opens, the Jews are citizens of a small province of the Syrian-Greek Empire; inspired by the fierce example of Mattathias, they take up arms against the unjust religious laws of Antiochus Epiphanes and his brutal desecration of the Temple; under Judas Maccabeus the Temple is recaptured and rededicated to the worship of the God of Israel; after Judas' death, his brother Jonathan, for all practical purposes, succeeds in driving the enemy out of Judea and is recognized by the Syrians as high priest; finally, under Simon, the Jews achieve peace and complete political independence with him as their high priest and civil ruler. This sketch should help to clarify some of the intricacies of the story.

The apparent complexity of the narrative is largely the result of the frequent introduction of the names of new generals and new kings among the Syrians, who were engaged in almost constant civil war after the death of Antiochus Epiphanes, rather than of any particular confusion in the course of events on the Jewish side. For the most part, the reader need make no attempt to keep track of these constantly shifting personalities. With such general facts in mind, it should be possible to read the story with a considerable degree of interest and understanding.

The opening verses of the book (1: 1-9) bring the history of the Greek Empire rapidly down from Alexander the

Great to the time of the Seleucid Emperor, Antiochus Epiphanes (roughly 333-175 B.C.). The first chapter then goes on to tell of the Hellenizers, that important group among the Jews, mostly of the upper classes, who were eager to give up their own ancestral religion for the religion and customs of the Greeks. Finally (1: 20ff), we hear of the beginning of the persecution under Antiochus Epiphanes. First, he plundered the Temple and then, two years later, began the policy of complete repression which eventually led to the revolt. The climax came, of course, when Antiochus forbade the practice of Judaism and desecrated the Temple by erecting the "abomination of desolation" (a heathen altar on which swine were sacrificed) upon the altar of Jehovah the God of Israel. The second chapter describes the violent reaction of the old priest, Mattathias, who, after slaying an apostate Jew and the king's officer, took his five strong sons and fled to the hills, where he was followed by a large part of the population, determined to die rather than give up their religion. Among those who joined him was a party called "the Assideans" (or "Hasidaeans"; Hebrew, "Chasidim"), the most devout of all the people of Israel and, on the whole, a pacifistic group, who favored putting reliance in God rather than in force of arms (2: 42). These are usually believed to be the ancestors of the Pharisees of the New Testament. Their willingness to join Mattathias' revolt was proof of the desperation to which the Jews had been reduced. Mattathias, on his deathbed, committed the great cause of defending the people of Israel and their faith to his son Judas, called Maccabeus, and the next section of the book (beginning at 3: 1) deals with the latter's amazing feats during the years which immediately followed.

Judas' initial victories over relatively small forces so enraged King Antiochus that he sent half his army under Lysias to defeat the upstarts, but the Jews continued to fight with such desperate tenacity of purpose that at the end of three years they were in control of most of Jerusalem and the Temple area and were able to cleanse the sacred precincts of the abominations which Antiochus had installed (4: 36-59). Although religious liberty was now re-established in Israel, the war continued, directed for the time being against the hostile neighbors of the Jews rather than against the Syrians (chap. 5).

Antiochus Epiphanes died during a campaign against the Parthians in the distant East (6: 1-16), but his successors and the various claimants to the throne who complicate so much of the subsequent history still tried to subjugate the turbulent Jews. During one of these battles, Eleazar, a brother of Judas, died a heroic death, crushed by a war elephant, an event which has always stirred the imagination of those who know the story of the Maccabees (6: 43-46). The elephant, a new instrument of warfare introduced from the East, was the frightening "secret weapon" of the Seleucid armies. At various times, the pressure of the Syrians relaxed, and when at last they sent Alcimus to be high priest, the Chasidim (Assidaeans) withdrew their support from Judas on the ground that they now had a high priest who could lay legitimate claim to the office (7: 13ff). The reader must remember that the Chasidim were pacifist in temper and had taken up arms only because no other way had seemed open at the moment.

In the eighth chapter we read that Judas made a treaty of alliance and friendship with the Romans. While the account may not be entirely accurate, it at least foreshadows the future course of events, for within a hundred years Judea was to be absorbed by the Roman Empire. Now, temporarily, the tide of Jewish victories began to subside, and in one of the later battles, Judas, deserted in cowardly fashion by a large part of his army, died (chap. 9).

Jonathan seized the reins relinquished by his fallen brother (9: 23-31), but soon discovered that his role was to be played rather in the field of intrigue than of battle, although the war still went on. John, one of Jonathan's two surviving brothers, was killed after being captured by the Arabs (9: 36-42). Jonathan was crafty enough to take full advantage of the struggle going on between Demetrius and Alexander Balas, two rival claimants to the Syrian throne, to get the best possible terms of peace. Both of them needed his support, but it was Alexander who made the highest bid, and fortunately it was he who was victor in the struggle for the kingdom. He appointed Jonathan both "Friend" of the king (a technical title) and high priest of the Jews (10: 18-20). Thus, in a period of about a dozen years, a son of Mattathias had fought his way up from the status of outlaw to that of trusted confidant and viceroy of the Syrian Emperor. Further dynastic rivalries and civil war within the Empire merely led to increased favor for the Jews (11: 28-37), since it was to the advantage of each new occupant of that most precarious throne to have the support of the courageous leader of Israel. But at last, Jonathan's good fortune changed. Tryphon, a courtier who was plotting rebellion against Antiochus VI, a king whom he himself had placed on the throne, seized Jonathan by treachery and eventually killed him (12: 39-48; 13: 23).

Thus, the last surviving brother, Simon, became high priest and chief of Israel's forces. Because of Tryphon's treachery he naturally entered into an alliance with Demetrius (II), Tryphon's chief opponent, and from him received a document granting complete independence to the Jews (13: 36-40). This led to a period of unparalleled peace and prosperity in Israel, a time celebrated in almost ecstatic language in 14: 4-15. As a reward for all that Simon and his brothers had done for the nation, the people made Simon hereditary high priest with all the power of civil government as well. He was called "high priest forever," words which remind us of Psalm 110, and some scholars believe this psalm was actually composed to celebrate his consecration to the office. In everything but name, Simon was the king, and one is not surprised to find that his grandson, Aristobulus I, assumed the name as well as the dignity.

The author of I Maccabees evidently intended to end his tale in a blaze of glory, and such is indeed the general effect. But he is too good a historian not to tell the whole truth, and part of the truth is that disintegration had begun. Now that the family of the Maccabees had a firm grip upon the reins of power, it was inevitable that intramural jealousy and intrigue, the curse of oriental kingship, should begin to appear. Simon did not meet his death at the hand of a foreign foe, but met it through the murderous design of his own son-in-law, who aimed to take his power from him (16: 11-17). It is well that the author determined to end his history with the death of Simon. The rest of the story, as we have already seen (p. 33 ff), is not a pretty one.

The concluding verses make it probable that the book was written after the death of John Hyrcanus (105 B.C.), the son and successor of Simon, but not too long after, since there is no mention of the kings who followed him. The author was evidently an admirer of the Hasmonean (Maccabean) family and wrote his history to tell of their wonderful accomplishments. His enthusiasm for the family of high priests makes it probable that he was of Sadducean sympathies and this supposition seems confirmed by the somewhat supercilious way in which he relates the story of the Chasidim (i.e. the Pharisees), as well as by his scrupulous avoidance of any reference to miracles or the Pharisees' doctrine of the resurrection of the dead. Although his religion was of the colder-blooded Sadducean variety, he was nevertheless a man of sincere and obvious piety. It is a part of his literary style to avoid using the name of God, but he uses "heaven" in the same sense (e.g., 4: 10, 24) as does St. Matthew's Gospel when it substitutes "Kingdom of Heaven" for the more customary "Kingdom of God." His book is written in the belief that loyalty to God and His covenant is required of every Jew and that God on His part will not desert those who put their trust in Him.

69

II Maccabees. This book is not a continuation of I Maccabees, but another account of some of the same events, with considerable expansion and an altogether different style and emphasis. Whether the author was acquainted with I Maccabees is still a subject of dispute among scholars, but it is at least possible he produced his own book in order to correct what seemed to him the defective religious point of view of the older history. The book is not based upon personal experience, nor is it the product of extensive scholarly research, but it is by the author's own confession merely an abridgment of a longer history, otherwise unknown to us, by a certain Jason of Cyrene (2: 23).

The main points which distinguish this book from I Maccabees are these: First, although II Maccabees begins its detailed history considerably before the time recorded by I Maccabees, it does not bring it down nearly so far. The author's story, as well as his personal admiration, is limited to Judas. He has nothing to say of the careers of Jonathan and Simon subsequent to the time of Judas and, as a matter of fact, does not even record the story of Judas' tragic end. He wants his story to have a happy ending and so bids farewell to his hero in the full flush of his victory over Nicanor. Second, whereas I Maccabees is straightforward, sober history, II Maccabees is composed with the pleasure and edification of the reader plainly in mind. That the author aimed to please is evident from his preface (2: 19-32) and his concluding postscript (15: 37-39); that he desired to convey religious inspiration rather than mere historical information is clear from his frequent mention of God, his love of the miraculous, and his painfully detailed accounts of the death of the martyrs. Third, if the author of I Maccabees can with some accuracy be described as a Sadducee because of his conservative religious attitude, the perfervid piety of the author of II Maccabees, together with his belief in angels and spirits and the resurrection of the dead, stamp him unmistakably as a Pharisee. Four, I Maccabees, as we have seen, was written in Hebrew, presumably in Palestine; II Maccabees was written in Greek and the prefatory letters make it almost certain that this took place in Egypt. If I Maccabees was composed early in the first century B.C., II Maccabees was certainly written later in the same century, but just when it is impossible to say.

The book we are considering, II Maccabees, opens with two letters (1: 1-10a and 1: 10b—2: 18) but the division between them is not clear in the King James version. They were allegedly written by the Jews of Palestine to the Jews of Egypt, and are mainly concerned with inducing the Egyptian Jews to join in the celebration of the Feast of Hanukkah (described curiously in 1: 9 as "the feast of tabernacles of the month Casleu [Chislev]," and in 2: 16 called "the purification"). The second letter contains an interesting legend about the altar fire of the Temple and a strange story about the prophet Jeremiah. Then follows the author's preface to his book, describing his sources and method (2: 19-32). The rest of the book is divided into two main parts: The first (3: 1—7: 42) relates the events which led up to the Maccabean revolt; the second (7: 43—15: 36) tells of the heroic career of Judas. The first episode is the attempt of Seleucus IV, the immediate predecessor of Antiochus Epiphanes, to plunder the Jerusalem temple. Informed of the fabulous treasure which the temple contained, he sent his emissary Heliodorus to obtain the funds, but this proved to be impossible because the attempted impiety of Heliodorus was frustrated by the sudden appearance of a heavenly horseman who drove him away (chap. 3). King Seleucus was succeeded by Antiochus Epiphanes, under whom the introduction of Greek customs among the Jews and the corruption of the priesthood—involving bribery, apostasy, and murder—increased at an alarming rate (chap. 4). Finally, with chapter 5, the book reaches the point at which the main story of I Maccabees begins, that is, the desecration of the temple by Antiochus Epiphanes and the proscription of the Jewish religion. After this, the main thread of the story is broken for two chapters (6 and 7) while the author introduces a considerable homiletic digression on the subject of martyrdom (6: 12-17), illustrated by two stories of martyrs, one of them told with an attention to gruesome details calculated to make the reader's flesh creep. First, there is the story of an old man, Eleazar, who refused to eat the flesh of swine and was condemned to death in consequence; then there is that of a mother and seven sons who were executed with terrifying cruelty for the same offense. Speeches are placed on the lips of each of them exhorting their fellow Jews to similar loyalty even though it may lead to the same kind of death.

Of special interest is the emphasis on the doctrine of a resurrection of the dead (7: 9, 14, 36; cf. 14: 46), which seems first to have become current with the Pharisees about this time. While there are anticipations of the idea in older parts of the Bible, it did not become a fixed doctrine in any form of Judaism until the frightful sufferings of devout Jews in the Maccabean age made such a belief seem necessary in order that men might hold fast to a belief in God's sovereignty and justice in a world apparently given over to the forces of evil. These stories are also interesting in that they mark the first appearance of the idea of martyrdom in religious literature, an idea which was to be of tremendous consequence in Christian thought, both in the New Testament (e.g. *Heb.* 11: 35) and in the first three Christian centuries. They provide the pattern for the martyr stories of the Early Christian Church.

With the outbreak of the Maccabean revolt, the main course of the narrative is resumed (chap. 8). The story told is essentially the same as that in I Maccabees with some divergence in details. Where the two accounts differ, I Maccabees is on the whole to be preferred. Most notable of such differences is that the death of Antiochus Epiphanes is said to have occurred before the rededication of the temple rather than afterwards. A comparison of the relatively sober account of the tyrant's end given in I Maccabees (6: 8-16) with the highly colored version of the same event which occupies the whole of II Maccabees 9 is very instructive as to the differences in the style, method, and mental outlook of the two authors. This section of the book reaches its climax in the story of the cleansing of the Temple and the establishment of the Feast of Hanukkah (10: 1-8).

Judas' continuing struggle with hostile neighbors and

with the successors of Antiochus Epiphanes is the theme of the rest of the book. In two of his battles, the intervention of angelic warriors saved the day (10: 29-30; 11: 8-10). Simon, whose glorious reign as high priest is the climax of I Maccabees, is barely mentioned in II Maccabees; and in one of the two meager references to his exploits, he is accused of covetousness (10: 20). This undoubtedly reflects the author's opinion of the Maccabean rulers who followed Judas; like the later Pharisees, he regarded the Hasmonean kings as mostly apostates and reprobates. Judas is his only hero.

Of particular importance in this part of the book is the reference to prayer and sacrifice for the dead (12: 43-45), the only mention of such a practice anywhere in the Bible although it became common in later Judaism and ultimately in Christianity. One does not have to accept the technical canonicity of II Maccabees in order to be glad that there is ancient warrant for a kind of prayer which seems so natural to the human heart and so congruous with the Biblical view of the after-life. The story of II Maccabees concludes with Judas' tremendous victories over the armies of Nicanor and the establishment of a second permanent feast, Nicanor's Day (15: 36; also mentioned in I Maccabees 7: 49). This feast continued to be observed by the Jews until the ninth century A.D.

The most impressive artistic monument to the Maccabees is Handel's great oratorio *Judas Maccabeus* with its stirring salute to the victor, "Hail, the conquering hero comes!"

III and IV Maccabees. The two books called III and IV Maccabees, which are found in editions of the Pseudepigrapha, have no direct connection with I and II Maccabees. III Maccabees purports to tell of a persecution of the Jews in the days of Ptolemy IV (222-204 B.C.), long before the time of the Maccabean revolt, and how they were delivered by a series of miraculous events. IV Maccabees is a retelling of the story of the martyrdoms related in II Maccabees (6: 18—7: 42) which makes use of the events to demonstrate the philosophical principle that reason is master of the passions. It is an important example of Hellenistic-Jewish philosophical writing. Neither of these books has ever been regarded as part of the standard Apocrypha of the Old Testament.

VI

TREATISES ON DIVINE AND HUMAN WISDOM: *ECCLESIASTICUS, WISDOM OF SOLOMON, BARUCH, THE EPISTLE OF JEREMY*, AND *THE PRAYER OF MANASSES*

Ecclesiasticus. Few men have deserved the epithet "scholar and gentleman" more than Jesus ben Sira, the author of the book strangely called Ecclesiasticus. His is the most human book in the Apocrypha and the only one whose author's name we know. This, in itself, is an indication that he speaks to us merely as man addressing man and not as an oracle of the Almighty. The modesty of his character is shown by his rejection of any claim to originality: "I awaked up last of all," he said, "as one that gathereth after the grapegatherers (33: 16)." But we must not take him too strictly at his word. It is true that he has no new doctrines to teach, but what he says is often expressed in striking and pungent fashion and one finds throughout his book the unique impress of a character most attractively compounded of deep religious feeling, wide human experience, profound culture, and a refreshing sense of humor. The book reveals him as one to whom nothing human or divine is alien and one whom we should like to know as friend and table companion as well as a guide to religious truth.

The prologue attributed to "an uncertain Author" which is printed in the King James Version is of no historical worth and may safely be ignored by the reader. On the other hand, the preface entitled "The Prologue of the Wisdom of Jesus the Son of Sirach" is historically reliable and contains several items of considerable interest. It was written by the author's grandson, who relates how he had moved to Egypt in 132 B.C. and there translated his grandfather's book from the original Hebrew into Greek.[1] He discusses the considerations which led him to undertake the translation and has some interesting comments on the difficulties of doing it.

The author, whose name Jesus is merely the Greek form of the common Old Testament named Joshua (Jeshua in Aramaic), was a citizen of Jerusalem, and from his book we learn a few scattered facts about him. He had traveled widely and, like St. Paul, had frequently suffered hardship and misadventure (34: 11-12; 51: 6). In common with other "wise men," he had served on diplomatic missions and was personally acquainted with life in the courts of kings (39: 4), although his regular occupation was that of

[1] Around the turn of the present century several manuscripts of Ecclesiasticus in Hebrew were discovered in the storeroom of an old synagogue in Cairo. They include about two-thirds of the book, but scholars are divided as to their value, although the authenticity of the text they contain seems now to have been confirmed by the discovery of part of a pre-Christian Hebrew scroll of Ecclesiasticus at Masada in Israel.

lecturer on religious and ethical subjects. For this purpose he conducted a regular school, a "house of learning," in Jerusalem (51: 23).

Ben Sira, as he is commonly called (the term means "son of Sira"), is a fine example of the class of men who gave us the canonical book of Proverbs as well as the somewhat unorthodox books of Ecclesiastes and Job.[2] Since we know more about him than any other of the wise men, we may take him for the prototype of them all. Certainly, he represents the main stream of the Wisdom tradition, soundly orthodox in religion and yet open to all the truth which comes from human experience and rational reflection upon it. Since he wrote before the outbreak of the persecution under Antiochus Epiphanes and the revolt which followed, his book breathes a serenity which would hardly be possible later on.

The proper name of the book is *The Wisdom of Jesus, the son of Sira* (or Sirach). The common name Ecclesiasticus, for which the author is in no way responsible, is something of a puzzle. The most probable explanation seems to be that it came to be called this because, in comparison with other apocryphal books, it was the ecclesiastical, or church, book *par excellence*, and was widely used in the Early Church as a manual of instruction in life and manners. Certainly, of all the books of the Apocrypha, it best justifies the pronouncement of the sixth Article of Religion on the value of the noncanonical books for this purpose.

[2] Robert C. Dentan, *The Holy Scriptures—A Survey* (New York: The Seabury Press), p. 97f.

Ecclesiasticus is divided into five main, but quite unequal, parts. Following the preface, the first and longest section (1: 1—42: 14) contains the "proverbs" of Ben Sira. This is a loose collection, almost entirely without organization, of the author's meditations and lectures on religious and ethical matters. It is strikingly similar to the main part of the book of Proverbs, although, for the most part, the discussions take the form of essays of considerable length rather than brief apothegms. The second section (42: 15—43: 33) is a poem praising God for His wonderful works in the world of physical nature. After that, it was only natural that the author should turn to the marvelous things God has wrought through human nature. This section (44: 1—49: 16), in which he recapitulates the history of the Hebrew people and the achievements of its great leaders, begins with the most familiar words in the book, "Let us now praise famous men, and our fathers that begat us!" It has a particular historical interest for readers of the New Testament since it provided the model for the great roll call of the heroes of faith in Hebrews 11. Finally, the last two chapters (50 and 51) are a kind of appendix. They contain, first of all, a poem in praise of the high priest Simon (not the Simon of I Maccabees, who came much later), which is of great interest as it contains the best description of the Temple services that has come down to us from Hebrew antiquity (50: 1-21). The prescriptions for the conduct of worship contained in the canonical Old Testament, for example in the book of Leviticus, are cold-blooded rubrics which are likely to bore, if not repel, the modern reader, but Ben Sira's flowery, but patently sincere words, introduce us to something of the rich emotion that found expression in Israel's traditional cult. The remaining brief sections of the appendix are personal and autobiographical and may be profitably read before embarking on a consecutive reading of the book.

The greatest difference between Ben Sira and the wise men who are responsible for our canonical book of Proverbs is in their attitude toward traditional religion. It has often been observed that the general course of the Wisdom movement in Israel was from secularism to religion, from philosophy to theology. In the context of Israel's life, it was impossible that any thinker of early times could have been completely secular, but a study of the book of Proverbs shows that the earliest elements in the book exhibit little attempt at making an explicit connection between Wisdom (that is, the pursuit of the good life) and Israel's unique religious faith. The later parts show a more definite concern with theological ideas and the motto finally written over the whole book is "The fear of the Lord (that is, religion) is the beginning of knowledge" (*Prov.* 1: 7). Even then the tendency was to think of religion in fairly general terms. It was Ben Sira who took the final step to bring Wisdom into complete conformity with the faith of Israel by identifying true Wisdom with the Law that God gave His people on Mount Sinai (19: 20; 24: 23). Ben Sira exemplifies the process of transition by which the old-fashioned, rather wordly minded, wisdom teacher of ancient Israel became the strictly religious student of the Law—the scribe of the New Testament, the rabbi of later times. His is a remarkably rich character in that it combines the cultured, secular wisdom of the older type with the fervid enthusiasm for the Law which would mark the newer. In this respect, his book constitutes a real bridge between the Testaments.

The modern reader is likely to be more interested in his worldly wisdom than in his rather conventional theology. A concern for physical health (30: 14-25) gives a curiously contemporary touch to his book, and the chapter in praise of physicians is unique in the Bible (38: 1-15). His essay on good manners at a dinner party has sometimes been regarded as an ancient prototype of modern books of etiquette and contains advice from which many of us can profit (31: 12—32: 13). As is to be expected in a man of his calling, Ben Sira was convinced of the superiority of the intellectual life (38: 24—39: 11), but he also had great respect for men who labor with their hands: "They will maintain the fabric of the world and in the handiwork of their craft is their prayer" (38: 34, Revised Version). His opinion of women is not high (25: 13-26; 26: 7-12), and some have supposed that a bitter personal experience may have soured him. But at the same time one must not forget that he classes a happy marriage among the chief blessings of life (25: 1; 26: 1-3, 13-18). In spite of his experience of the world and his taste for cultivated society, he is, like all the wise men, an advocate of the simple life: "The chief thing for life is water, and bread, and clothing, and an house to cover shame" (29: 21).

Ben Sira's philosophy of education seems decidedly unenlightened to the modern reader, especially to one who has been affected by the theories of progressive education.

He knows no method but that of stern discipline (30: 1-13). "Cocker thy child, and he shall make thee afraid; play with him, and he will bring thee to heaviness" (30: 9). In this, of course, he is merely a man of his times, reflecting the prevailing view. He fully recognizes the tragedy of much of human life (40: 1-8), but on the whole finds the world a good and pleasant place in which to live (40: 18-27).

Although Ben Sira had no great contribution to make to Israel's religious thinking, certain of his ideas are of considerable interest from the historical point of view. With all of his deep religious feeling, he was content to walk in the old ways and, for that reason, would have to be classified as a Sadducee. There is no place in his philosophy for angels, spirits, or a life after death: "The son of man is not immortal" (17: 30). The practical character of his piety is shown by his emphasis on good works (29: 1-20) and especially on almsgiving: "Water will quench a flaming fire; and alms maketh an atonement for sins" (3: 30). It will be remembered that the book of Tobit places a similar emphasis upon almsgiving and that the New Testament takes it for granted as one of the major duties of religion. While he believes that the written Law is the embodiment of wisdom and counsels a high regard for the clergy (7: 29-31), he is opposed to superstition and to the substitution of pious practices for ethical living (7: 9, 14; 34: 18—35: 3).

Ben Sira deals with so many subjects that it is impossible, adequately, to summarize his thought. As is the case with most of the non-narrative books of the Bible, Ecclesiasticus should be read slowly, a little at a time, and the reader should stop frequently to savor its full aroma.

Wisdom of Solomon. If Ecclesiasticus is chiefly interesting to us for its wisdom in the field of ethics and general human conduct, the Wisdom of Solomon, by contrast, is of interest almost exclusively for its theology. It is the great theological treatise of the Apocrypha and is indeed one of the great theological books of the Bible. For dramatic purposes it is written in the form of an essay by King Solomon, but the disguise is a transparent one, and it is doubtful that it was ever intended to be taken seriously. From early times, the book was recognized as pseudonymous, but this has never caused any serious student to undervalue its importance. Most readers will agree that the Apocrypha is worth keeping in our Bibles for the sake of this one book, if for nothing else.

A few scholars still defend the thesis that the book, or at least the first part of it, was written in Hebrew, but the common view is that it was written in Greek from the very beginning. Certainly, it is suffused with the Greek spirit and the Greek way of thinking as is no other book in the Bible. It represents the first great attempt to make a synthesis between the insights of Greek philosophy and the great truths of Biblical revelation. From this book we get a glimpse of a kind of Judaism altogether different in temper and outlook from the rather conventional piety of Ecclesiasticus or the ardent nationalism of Judith or the introverted legalism of the scribes and Pharisees of the

New Testament period. The groups in the ancient world who were most accessible to the preaching of the Gospel of Christ were, on the one hand, Jews who had been influenced by Hellenism and, on the other, Greeks who had been influenced by Judaism. It was in Alexandria that this fusion of cultures first began to take form and the Wisdom of Solomon is its greatest monument. It was known to the writers of the New Testament and exerted considerable influence upon them.

Although the author had been deeply affected by Greek thought, he was a thoroughly orthodox Jew and was greatly disturbed at the spectacle of some, perhaps many, of his race who had deserted the religion of their ancestors and had become profligate in their manner of life as well as pagan in their way of thought. The purpose of his book was to win them back to the true wisdom which had been the guiding star of Israel's national existence. The book attempts to do this in three different ways, corresponding to its three major divisions: First of all, the lot of the righteous man who follows Wisdom is shown to be vastly superior to that of the ungodly (1:1—6: 11); then follows a long section in the form of a hymn in praise of Wisdom, which is pictured as the artificer and orderer of the whole created cosmos (6: 12—9: 18). The last, longest, and least satisfactory part of the book is an effort to show how glorious the history of the Jewish people had been and how God's providence had watched over them all the way (10: 1—19: 22). Curiously enough, the idea of Wisdom occurs only in the brief opening chapter of this section (10: 1— 11: 1) and even the word Wisdom occurs but once in the remainder of the book. The whole section from 11: 2 to the end is so different from the previous chapters that many scholars have supposed it to have been written by a different hand. However, in spite of all the differences, there are striking points of similarity and it is entirely possible that a single author, like many others before and after him, simply found that the spring of inspiration, which had flowed so abundantly when he began his book, tended to fail in the latter part of his task. In any case, the general reader should be aware that, while the section which begins in 11: 2 contains some passages of considerable historical and theological interest, it is not on the whole as rewarding as the first ten chapters of the book.

The book begins with an address to the kings and potentates of earth, admonishing them to follow the ways of the Lord. This manner of opening is required by the fiction that Solomon is the author and is addressing his equals. After the opening verse, the author forgets his disguise and does not assume it again until the peroration which concludes Part I (6: 1-11). His remarks in between are obviously intended for any reader who has eyes to see and ears to hear. The main argument may be summarized in the thought that unrighteousness results in death, whereas goodness leads to eternal life.

In the opening chapter there appears an idea which is entirely new in the Old Testament tradition: that man is by nature immortal and that it was only sin which brought death into the world. The second chapter epitomizes the views of the hedonistic Jews who had fallen victim to the temptations of a false pagan philosophy. They are represented as arguing, in words which have a strangely modern ring, that since life has no meaning or purpose and death is the end of everything, one should seize the moment and indulge the physical senses to the full. From this line of reasoning it follows further that "might is right" and that one is foolish to allow his actions to be controlled by any sentimental regard for the poor and helpless. The beginning of this discussion (2:1-6) runs so closely parallel to the thought of the canonical Ecclesiastes that it seems probable the author actually had that most curious of Old Testament books in mind and intended his own book to be, at least in part, a refutation of its argument. In one paragraph of this chapter (2: 12-20) the author describes the oppression of the righteous in language which strikingly suggests the sufferings of Jesus and was naturally taken by the early Church as a prophecy of the Passion. Needless to say, the resemblance is merely a coincidence, except in so far as we can say that our Lord's crucifixion perfectly exemplified the character and meaning of all innocent suffering.

The climax of this section comes in chapter 3 which opens with the most famous words of the book: "The souls of the righteous are in the hand of God." Here for the first time in Old Testament literature we find a thoroughly developed conception of personal immortality and of perfect happiness for all the righteous in a life beyond the grave. Even in the book of Daniel, where the idea of the resurrection of the dead first appears, it is only a selected group ("many of them") which is to be raised (*Dan.* 12: 2).

In the book of Wisdom immortality is the natural lot of all righteous men. The wicked are apparently doomed to extinction (3: 17, 18). Although the ideas expressed in this chapter may accurately be described as a logical development of certain basic premises laid down in the canonical Old Testament, particularly in the area of the Old Testament doctrine of God, yet it is interesting, and historically significant, that these conclusions are expressed in language borrowed from Greek philosophy. The word *immortality* (3: 4) is only the most obvious example. The remainder of the first part of the book merely amplifies the thought already announced in 3: 1. It is of incidental interest to note that the imagery of the "armor of salvation" used in Ephesians 6: 13-17 is obviously borrowed from Wisdom 5: 17-19 (which in turn is based on Isaiah 59: 17).

The praise of Wisdom which occupies the second part of the book (6: 12—9: 18) represents the highest development of the idea of Wisdom to be found in Jewish religious literature. The general treatment was suggested by the eighth chapter of Proverbs, but what in Proverbs is merely poetry has here become metaphysical doctrine. Wisdom is pictured as the mediator, in some sense, between God and the cosmos, the Divine Idea by which the world was made and through which it is sustained. Wisdom is the principle of order which runs through the whole of the created universe; the natural world is regulated by her influence, and man must learn to regulate his life by her as well. Although Wisdom is consistently personified throughout the description, it is doubtful that the author intended the reader to understand that she was really a person. On the whole, his idea most resembles the Stoic conception of the logos, which was that of an impersonal principle. The language of Wisdom 7: 22—8: 1 is strikingly reminiscent of the language of the Stoic philosophers. Some time after the book of Wisdom was written (probably in the first century B.C., although some scholars put it as late as the first century A.D.), the Alexandrian Jewish philosopher Philo used the same idea, but preferred the Greek word *logos* (which means "word" or "reason") rather than the Hebrew word *hokhma* which we translate "Wisdom." If one will recall the use of the expression "word" (that is *logos*) in John 1: 1-14, he will see that the author of the Fourth Gospel was writing in the tradition represented by Philo and the book of Wisdom. Other New Testament passages which show the unmistakable influence of Wisdom 7: 22—8: 1 are Colossians 1: 15-17 and Hebrews 1: 2-3. In the familiar Advent hymn, "O come, O come, Emmanuel" the second verse contains a paraphrase of Wisdom 8: 1:

> O come, thou Wisdom from on high,
> Who orderest all things mightily.
> (Hymn 2, *The Hymnal, 1940*)

In Part II, the author resumes his pretended role of King Solomon (6: 12—7: 21 and 8: 2-21), but in the third part of the book the character of Solomon disappears altogether. The theme of this section (chapters 10-19) is the superiority of Israel as shown in her history. If chapter 10 can be regarded as an integral part of what follows, then the motif may be regarded as Wisdom's providential care of Israel.

The purpose of the author in writing this section will be evident if we remember that throughout the whole book he is endeavoring to win apostate Jews to the faith of their fathers. The most interesting part of the section is the essay on the nature and folly of idolatry in chapters 13-15, especially since the first part of the discussion (13: 1-9) seems to be the basis of St. Paul's famous treatment of natural theology in Romans 1: 20-21. The book of Wisdom argues eloquently that all men have the power to know God from the beauty and power of the visible world; St. Paul accepted this line of reasoning and consequently maintained that the Gentiles had always had the possibility of knowing the true God and therefore could not escape moral responsibility for their vicious lives and the perversity of their religious practices.

The magnanimity which characterizes the author of Wisdom is nowhere better shown than in his sympathetic analysis of the mind of the pagan world. He distinguishes between two kinds of idolatry: There is first that which consists in a worship of the wonders of nature—the sun, the moon or the stars—and which is excusable because, at least, it is directed toward objects which are great and beautiful and can lead the mind of the intelligent man upward toward the worship of "the first author of beauty" who is "the maker of them" (13: 3 and 5). But he can find no excuse for those who, with incredible stupidity, actually worship human or animal images which their own hands have made (13: 10 and following). Like Paul, he finds in the false theology of the pagan world the source of its moral corruption (14: 12).

Baruch and the Epistle of Jeremy. The last book which can be included in the category of Wisdom literature is the so-called book of Baruch, in which the Epistle of Jeremy (actually a separate book) now appears as a sixth chapter. The book in its present form purports to be a letter addressed by Baruch, the friend and secretary of Jeremiah, from his exile in Babylon to the Jews left in Jerusalem after the beginning of the Babylonian captivity. It is intended to induce in its hearers a mood of quiet submission to the conquering power (notice the advice to pray for the royal family of Babylon [1: 11, 12]), to summon them to repentance for the sins which had brought calamity upon them, and, finally, to awaken in them a sense of faith in God's ultimate purpose to deliver his people and restore the holy city. Since the book obviously has a practical purpose and many internal indications show that it cannot actually have been written at the time of the Babylonian exile, one naturally wonders what particular situation called it forth. Scholars are divided in the answers they give. Some would connect it with the persecution under Antiochus Epiphanes, while others believe it was written after the destruction of the temple by the Romans in A.D. 70. Even if the latter date should prove to be correct, the book is certainly composed in part of older materials which may go back several centuries. The original language was undoubtedly Hebrew, although only the Greek translation survives.

The book falls naturally into three parts: The first (1: 1—3: 8) consists of the supposed letter of Baruch (1: 1-14), which alone gives unity to the book, and the litur-

TREATISES ON DIVINE AND HUMAN WISDOM

gical confession and prayers which follow it; the second part (3: 9—4: 4), which justifies us in including the book in a chapter on Wisdom Literature, is a brief essay (poetic in the original Hebrew) which attributes Israel's sufferings to her apostasy from "the fountain of Wisdom." The poet agrees with the author of Job 28 that ultimate Wisdom can be known only to God, but asserts with Ben Sira that, in the Law of Moses, God has revealed the essence of this Wisdom to men (4: 1). The final section (4: 5—5: 9), probably also poetry in the original, brings encouragement to the people and a promise of the final restoration of Zion. Chapter 4: 5-35 is marked by the recurrent refrain "be of good cheer," or its equivalent (see vss. 5, 21, 27, and 30), and the section 4: 30—5: 9 by the regular repetition of "O Jerusalem." The book of Baruch has no particular historical or religious value. Its chief interest is in showing us that, even in very late times, a period of national adversity could produce literature of comfort in the sober tradition of the older prophets, as well as the extravagances of the newer apocalyptic.

Originally a separate book in the Septuagint, the so-called Epistle of Jeremy came to be attached to the book of Baruch because of the historical fact that Baruch and the prophet Jeremiah were close friends and associates. The letter is certainly not by Jeremiah, but nothing can be said with any confidence about its real author, or even about the date and original language. It consists of a rambling polemic against idolatry, but of a far lower and much less imaginative character than that in Wisdom 13-15. Like the preceding two chapters of Baruch, it has a refrain, occurring at irregular intervals, "they are no gods; fear them not," which may also be taken as a motto for the entire work (See vss. 16, 23, 29, 65 and 69).

II Baruch. Among the Pseudepigrapha there is a book called II Baruch. It has no relation to the apocryphal book described here beyond the fact that both are attributed to the same author. It is an apocalyptic work which comes from the same period as II Esdras and has many affinities with it. II Baruch is one of the most important and attractive of the non-Christian apocalyptic writings.

The Prayer of Manasses. In II Chronicles 33: 10-13 it is related that Manasseh, the wickedest of the Kings of Judah, was taken captive by the Assyrians and underwent a profound conversion while in prison. The little book called The Prayer of Manasses professes to be the prayer of penitence which he uttered there. Its date is probably about the beginning of the Christian era; the author is, of course, unknown. It is of interest chiefly as a dignified example of an ancient Jewish penitential prayer.

VII

AN IMPORTANT APOCALYPSE: II ESDRAS

It is fortunate, for bridging the gulf between the Testaments, that among the books included in our English Apocrypha there is one example of a fully developed apocalypse. For most people, the book of Revelation is the most difficult book in the New Testament to understand. It cannot be understood at all unless we see it against its background and realize that it belongs to a whole class of literature which arose in times of persecution and continued to be popular for several centuries. This literature we call apocalyptic, because it purports to give a revelation (in Greek, *apocalypsis*) of the future. The apocalypses vary considerably in details, but all agree in saying that the present evil time will pass and God's kingdom will soon be established. Sometimes, they picture the coming of a conqueror—the Messiah—who will win the victory on God's behalf; sometimes they represent God as establishing His rule by Himself without the intervention of a Messianic figure. Sometimes the future history of the world is told in relatively simple fashion, as in the book of Daniel; sometimes it is extremely complicated, as in the New Testament book of Revelation.

In any case, the modern reader must not take the detailed predictions too seriously. Instead, he should think of these books as poetry which presents in dramatic, imaginative, and often fantastic, form the single theme of the ultimate certainty of God's triumph over the forces of evil. Most of the apocalypses are pseudonymous: that is, they are attributed to some ancient worthy such as Daniel, Enoch, Baruch, or, in the case of our present book, Ezra, rather than to their actual authors. All the apocalypses speak a more or less common language of symbols; the same stock figures recur in most of them. Finally, most of the apocalypses are composite: that is, they are composed of older writings which have been fused together into a single more or less consistent whole. Since every apocalypse conforms in some degree to this customary pattern, it is evident that the more widely one reads apocalyptic literature in general, the better he will understand any particular representative of the type. For this reason II Esdras is a very useful book for increasing our understanding of Revelation and other apocalyptic passages in the New Testament.

The process by which II Esdras was composed was a particularly complicated one extending over a period of some two hundred years. Disregarding for the moment the borrowings from a common stock of older apocalyptic materials, we find that the various sections of the book in

its present form date from the first to the third centuries
A.D. The dates just mentioned, all in the Christian era, will
explain a curious fact which has struck every reader who
ever started to examine the book as it appears in our
English Apocrypha: namely, that certain portions are
obviously Christian, not Jewish. For example 2: 42-48 describes Jesus and the early Christian martyrs and in 7: 28
our Lord is actually mentioned by name! The book as we
find it in our Apocrypha was never known to Jewish readers, although in an older form it certainly was.

The version in the English Bible does not come to us
directly from the Greek (for the very good reason that
the Greek version no longer exists!) but from a late and
corrupt Latin manuscript. There are other versions in
various oriental languages but none of these have the dis-
tinctively Christian elements which were added to the book
in the course of the second and third century after Christ.
Chapters 1 and 2 were probably added in the second century; chapters 15 and 16 in the third. Other minor inter-
polations in the text of the book (such as the name Jesus
in 7: 28) may have occurred about the same time or even
later. Since our chief interest is naturally in the oldest form
of the book, the reader is advised, at least the first time
through, to skip the Christian additions and confine his
reading to chapters 3-14, which (minus the small inter-
polations previously referred to) constitute the old Jewish
apocalypse.

Even in these chapters, it is evident that we are not
dealing with a homogeneous work. Chapters 3-13 belong
together and contain the visions of a certain Salathiel

(identified by an editor as being also Ezra); chapter 14 is an entirely independent narrative which tells how Ezra in the days after the Babylonian exile miraculously preserved the books of the Law. It is generally agreed that these sections really have nothing to do with each other and that Salathiel originally had no connection with Ezra. The note that Salathiel was also Ezra (3: 1) was added when some editor joined the two parts together.[1] But the Salathiel chapters themselves are not a unity; even the reader who is not used to this kind of material will see that there is a great difference between the four visions of chapters 3-10 in which Salathiel (Ezra) discusses with the angel his doubts about the justice of God, and the two strictly apocalyptic visions of the Eagle in chapters 11-12 and the Son of Man in 13. It is evident that even the Salathiel apocalypse, as we have it, is the result of a considerable process of development. The New Testament book of Revelation is probably also such a composite work and, if so, this explains much of its complexity and apparent inconsistency.

Lest the reader should feel hopelessly confused at this point, it may be well to summarize our discussion by listing the various elements of the book in consecutive outline form: Chapters 1-2, a late Christian addition to the original Jewish book; chapters 3-13, the Salathiel Apocalypse (chapters 4-10 containing his visionary discussions with the angel Uriel, and chapters 11 through 13 containing the Eagle

---

[1] The reference to Ezra and Salathiel, correctly given in the Revised Version and in Goodspeed, is unfortunately omitted in the King James Version.

and Son of Man visions); chapter 14, the Ezra legend; and chapters 15-16, another late Christian addition.

Even when the Christian material has been eliminated, the Jewish Apocalypse which remains is still the latest book in the Apocrypha, later than most of the books of the New Testament itself. We study it today not because it had any direct influence on the New Testament, but because it shows the kind of forces which were stirring in New Testament times and illustrates a type of thinking which was shared by several New Testament writers. While part of the book goes back to the events which culminated in the fall of Jerusalem in A.D. 70, other parts seem to come from the reign of Domitian in the last two decades of the first century, or even later, and thus from the general period which produced the New Testament book of Revelation. Of course, II Esdras was never included in the Septuagint. It and the Prayer of Manasses do not come into the English Apocrypha from the Greek Bible, but from the appendix to the Latin Vulgate, where it is called IV Esdras.

It is obviously impossible here to do any more than summarize in a very general way the contents of this strange, but fascinating, book. One must frankly admit that the reader who comes to it for the first time is likely to find the strangeness more evident than the fascination. Most of it may seem fantastic, irrelevant, and extremely confusing. But to those who have patience to persevere and a desire to understand, apocalyptic literature such as this can contribute much by heightening religious feeling and stimulating the religious imagination. We are introduced to Salathiel, the hero of the first part of the book in 3: 1

(Revised Version), where he is also identified as Esdras (Ezra). Since Salathiel is well known in the Bible as a member of the Jewish royal family and the father of Zerubbabel (*I Esd.* 5: 5 and *Matt.* 1: 12; *Luke* 3: 27 [Shealtiel is the same as Salathiel]), it is obvious that he could not also have been Ezra, who lived about one hundred years later. So we are justified in ignoring the references to Ezra throughout this part of the book. As noted above, they were put in when chapter 14, which *is* about Ezra, was added to the original apocalypse.

In chapters 3-10, Salathiel is represented as being chiefly concerned with the problem of God's justice. He acknowledges that all men have been wicked from the very beginning; in Adam's sin we have all sinned (3: 21-22). This is the first known appearance of the doctrine of original sin in Jewish literature (the canonical Old Testament teaches that Adam was the first sinner, but nowhere says his guilt was shared by, or transmitted to, his descendants). Since all have sinned, all deserve punishment, but why (says Salathiel) should Israel, the chosen people of God, suffer so much more than the heathen, who had no special relationship to God and whose deeds were so much worse than Israel's (3: 32-33)?

The problem—that of the suffering of the innocent—is a perennial one, first raised in an acute form by the author of the book of Job, and is still with us today. Of all the books in the Bible, only Job shows a greater concern with the problem of life's apparent injustice than the Salathiel apocalypse. In a series of three visions (3: 1—5: 19; 5: 20—6: 34; 6: 35—9: 25), the angel Uriel (meaning "God is my

ight") comes to deal with his difficulties. The angel's
ine of reasoning is twofold: in the first place he declares
that mere man cannot hope to understand the mind of God.
God moves in His mysterious ways His wonders to per-
form (4: 10-21)!

Salathiel's hesitance to accept this answer has a very
modern sound to it (4: 12 and 22-23). But the angel has
another argument, namely, that the end of the world and
the last judgment are not far off and in the long run the
righteous will be vindicated (4: 26 and following). In the
two later visions, this double line of argument is extended
and elaborated. In the third vision (beginning at 6: 35),
we meet with the figure of the Messiah (in the present form
of the book explicitly identified with Jesus—7: 28), who is
to live on earth for four hundred years and then die. After
that the resurrection (7: 28-32) will come. (If the reader
compares the King James Version of the Apocrypha with
that of the Revised Version, he will notice that the latter
includes seventy extra verses between 7: 35 and 36 of the
King James Version. The lost verses are inserted from an
ancient Latin manuscript rediscovered in 1875.) In the
fourth vision (9: 26 and following), Uriel shows Salathiel
a vision of the restored Jerusalem of the future.

Chapters 11-12 contain a vision of quite different character, that of an eagle rising from the sea to dominate the
whole world. This is plainly a picture of the Roman Empire, which our book identifies with the last of the four
beasts mentioned in Daniel 7 (*II Esd.* 11: 39 and 12: 11).
The student of the times can recognize many historical
illusions in this picture, but part of it has become so con-

fused through the book having been altered to meet new situations that the full sense can no longer be recovered. The main point is that the Empire is approaching its end and is to be overthrown by the Messiah, who will come to vindicate God's people (12: 31-32). Another and more elaborate picture of the redemptive activity of the Messiah is given in chapter 13 where he is described as one "in the likeness of a man" (13: 3, Revised Version; Daniel's Son of Man, *Dan.* 7: 13) whose task is to rescue all the tribes of Israel from the hand of their oppressors. Both these visions give us a clear picture of the political nature of the Messianic idea and help us to understand why the disciples could ask Jesus such questions as when he intended to restore the kingdom to Israel.

In the last chapter of the Jewish part of the book (14), there is a remarkable legend about Ezra. Here, at last, Ezra (Esdras in Greek) appears in his own right. The story is that the Babylonians had destroyed the books of the Old Testament, but Ezra, through divine inspiration, was able to restore them all, dictating them to his secretaries over a period of forty days (14: 39-44; the Revised Version is correct in verse 44). In addition to the canonical books, he dictated seventy others which were not to be published, but kept only for the eyes of a few initiates (45-48). These seventy books are, of course, such books as II Esdras, and the story is intended to explain, among other things, why such a book as this, supposedly written centuries before, could only just have come to light.

The most difficult book in the Apocrypha for the modern reader to understand and appreciate is II Esdras but, like the other apocalypses, it is the product of a religious faith which was being tested in the fire of adversity and cannot be brushed impatiently aside as though it were some rather unpleasant fairy tale. To understand it in any measure is to be given a new appreciation of the power of the human spirit to create visions of hope in the midst of black despair. While modern man can hardly learn to speak again the language of apocalyptic, he will certainly wish that he might express in the language of his own day, either by poetry or prose, the sublime faith which such writers had in the ultimate triumph of the kingdom of God.

VIII

WHAT WE LEARN FROM

THE APOCRYPHA

In this last chapter we shall survey in summary fashion a few of the areas which receive special illumination from the Apocrypha. This is the kind of information which justifies us in calling it the Bridge of the Testaments.

Political History. In the last of the Old Testament historical books the Jews are seen as citizens of the Persian Empire. From I—II Maccabees we learn they later passed under Greek rule, rose in savage revolt against Antiochus Epiphanes, and eventually achieved a short-lived independence under the Hasmonean kings. While these books do not relate the events which led to the rise of Herod and the establishment of the Roman Empire in Palestine, there are numerous references to the Romans in I Maccabees and the perceptive reader can see the shadow of coming events cast long before.

Sects and Parties. The Apocrypha also illustrates the rise of the principal parties which were to divide the Jews of New Testament times.

I The Pharisees: I Maccabees introduces us to the Chasidim, the "pious ones," who were the forerunners of the Pharisees and perhaps of other strange sects of first century Palestine such as the Essenes, of whom we learn in the writings of Josephus. The recently discovered Dead Sea Scrolls seem to have belonged to the library of some devout, but eccentric, sect such as this. The violent Maccabean Age was a fertile breeding ground for all kinds of new movements and extravagant ideas. The Chasidim were, as I Maccabees shows, basically pacific in temper. Although bitterly opposed to foreign rule in any form, they trusted in God to deliver them and joined the revolt of Judas only as a last desperate measure. In New Testament times the Pharisees, as we know from sources outside the Bible, exhibited the same attitude toward Roman rule. The second book of Maccabees, which lays so much emphasis upon supernatural intervention in human affairs, seems to be written from their point of view.

II The Sadducees: On the other hand, I Maccabees appears to be essentially Sadducean in outlook. It has nothing to say of miraculous deliverances, stresses the human achievements of its heroes and reaches its climax in glorifying the rule of Simon, the Maccabean high priest. As is well known, the Sadducees of the New Testament period were the high-priestly party (and, incidentally, inclined to be friendly toward the Romans, as many of the high priest's party had been friendly to the Greeks in the days of Antiochus Epiphanes). The conservative Sadducean point of view is also represented by Ben Sira, the author of Ecclesiasticus, who emphasizes human free will and moral responsibility, denies man's immortality, and closes his book with a paean of praise to the high priest.

III The Zealots: Finally, the book of Judith evidences the presence in certain rigidly orthodox circles of a kind of fanaticism, engendered by long foreign oppression, which could regard assassination as a legitimate weapon against Israel's enemies. This spirit persisted in later times and increased in violence. In the first century A.D. it led to the formation of the Zealot party, dedicated to the forcible overthrow of Roman rule, and to the rise of the Sicarii (the "murderers" or "assassins" of Acts 21: 38) who regarded the daggers they habitually hid under their cloaks as the most effective tools for driving the alien from the land.

A knowledge of the tremendous heat generated by these mutually antagonistic parties with their differing attitudes toward foreign rule gives added point to the question asked of Jesus: "Is it lawful for us to give tribute unto Caesar, or no?" and provides a background for a better understanding of the circumstances which led to His crucifixion.

The Doctrine of God. Although the essential structure of Old Testament religion remained unaltered in the period covered by the Apocrypha, certain aspects of it underwent important modifications. One notes particularly that the doctrine of God changed in the direction of emphasizing His transcendence, that is, His remoteness from the world. A tendency in this direction is already apparent in the canonical Old Testament where the thoughtful reader is well aware of the gulf which separates the God of the J-document, who "walks in the garden in the cool of the day" (*Gen.* 3: 8), from the majestic God of Second Isaiah, whose thoughts are not our thoughts and whose ways are not our ways (*Isa.* 55: 8). The author of I Maccabees shows this tendency in one way by omitting the name of God in his book. He did this, certainly not because he was an irreligious man, but presumably because he regarded God's name as too holy to be introduced into a mere book of human history. While later Jews rarely went to this extreme of reticence, the rabbis often preferred to use some circumlocution such as Heaven, the Shekinah, or the Name, rather than baldly use the word God. The occasional substitution of Heaven in the New Testament for God (as in the phrase Kingdom of Heaven) is a result of this same tendency.

Angels and Demons. More important than this avoidance of the divine name, which appears in only one of the Apocryphal books, is the introduction of angels as intermediaries between God and man, so as to remove God from direct contact with His world. While angels occasionally appear in the Old Testament, they have little significance and there is nothing in the nature of angelology outside the book of Daniel (which is, of course, contemporary with the earlier literature of the Apocrypha). In the Apocrypha there is a well-developed angelology which is particularly evident in II Maccabees, Tobit, and II Esdras. In these books angelic help is taken for granted as one of the regular resources of the religious man. In this period we first meet with angels who have proper names: Michael and Gabriel in Daniel, and Raphael and Uriel in Tobit and II Esdras. Along with angels, we learn from Tobit of the existence of demons. The demon of Tobit has a proper name, Asmodeus, as do the demons of the gospel story who declare their name is Legion.

Wisdom and Logos. The need to discover some means of mediating between the transcendent God and His world takes a more philosophical form in the developed concept of Wisdom which is so important a feature of the Wisdom of Solomon (especially 7: 22—8: 1). Students of Christian theology have always recognized in the Alexandrian Wisdom (or Logos) idea the basic material from which part of the New Testament doctrine of the nature of Christ was formed.

The Law. The idea of God's Law in the period of the canonical Old Testament was a developing concept which even in the latest books hardly meant all that St. Paul means when he condemns reliance on "the works of the Law" (for example, Galatians 2: 16). It is in the inter-testamental period that the full development of the legal religion of "the scribes and Pharisees" took place. This is most apparent in Ecclesiasticus and Baruch, where the Law which was given to Moses on Mount Sinai is said to be the sum total of all the Wisdom accessible to man. The book of Judith shows to what fanatical extremes the idea of devotion to the Law can be carried and helps one understand Paul's reaction against the whole idea that one can become righteous by meticulously fulfilling its commands.

Many find a different attitude toward the Law in II Esdras. Parts of the "Salathiel Apocalypse" (see p. 95 f) express a pessimistic view of human nature which includes even those who live under the Law (for example, II Esdras 8: 35). While the Law is regarded as Israel's unique and precious possession, it seems to inspire the author of these passages with no sense of elation or self-confidence. Deliverance out of man's present evil state, according to his philosophy, must come from God alone, not from the observance of the Law. It would seem from this that there were other Jews of the New Testament age who shared St. Paul's dissatisfaction with legalistic Judaism.

Life After Death. The greatest change in the religion of the Jews took place in the realm of belief in an after-life. For the typical man of the canonical Old Testament, birth and death were the farthest horizons. For the new man of the later inter-testamental period, who knew the miseries of life in a world apparently dominated by the powers of evil, there had been opened the vision of a life beyond death in which the inequities of the present age would be corrected. Not all the writers of the Apocrypha shared this hope— Ben Sira and the author of I Maccabees, like the New Testament Sadducees, certainly did not—but it appears full blown in II Maccabees, II Esdras, and Wisdom (as, of course, also in Daniel and the so-called Isaiah apocalypse [*Isa.* 24-27, see 26: 19], both from the late Greek period).

In Wisdom it takes the form of a belief in the Greek concept of the immortality of the soul; in the other books it has the Semitic and more Biblical form of a belief in the actual resurrection of the body. This is the form it also has on the lips of Martha, when she declares, with regard to her brother Lazarus, "I know that he shall rise again in the resurrection at the last day" (*John* 11: 24).

The Messiah. Along with a belief in the resurrection of the dead there naturally went a belief in the coming of a Messiah, an "anointed one," who would establish God's kingdom on earth. Curiously enough, since we know the idea was widely held, only one book of the Apocrypha contains it, namely, II Esdras. There, however, in chapters 11-13 it appears in a fully developed form such as must have been very common in certain Jewish circles in the first century A.D. After reading this book we can understand the anxiety with which the question would be asked: "Art thou he that should come or do we look for another?" (*Matt.* 11: 3) We also see from this book how the close connection of the Messianic concept with nationalistic and political ideas made it impossible for most Jews to recognize the very different character of the Messiah who actually came.

Apocalyptic. The importance of II Esdras for an understanding of apocalyptic has been sufficiently emphasized in the chapter which deals with that book. Here we need only remind ourselves of the significance of the Maccabean revolt for the whole subject of Apocalyptic Literature. The latter part of Daniel would be a closed book to us if it were not for our knowledge of the events related in the books of Maccabees, and since all later apocalypses depend on Daniel, they too would be largely unintelligible. The arrangement of the present American Prayer Book lectionary takes account of this relationship between Daniel and Maccabees by having us read the two books in conjunction. On the Saturday before the fourth Sunday after Trinity, Episcopalians are directed to begin the reading of I Maccabees at Evening Prayer, and then nearly two weeks later, when they have finished the fourth chapter with its account of the re-dedication of the Temple, they begin the reading of the book of Daniel, which was written shortly after that event. In this way the Church makes it easier for us to understand Daniel, since we read it in its proper historical setting.

Original Sin. The canonical Old Testament indulges in almost no speculation on the metaphysical origin of sin, either in the individual or in the race, although it tells us that Adam was the first sinner. Later ages were not content with so pragmatic a view. For Ben Sira, sin was an unhappy legacy from our first parent and the cause of death (*Ecclus.* 25: 24), but the thought came to him only incidentally and was never developed further. On the other hand, II Esdras, somberly pessimistic, sees the world as a very evil place in which all men go about laden with a burden of guilt inherited from Adam (*II Esd.* 3: 21-22; 7: 48). This is the first Jewish book to our knowledge that contains a fully articulated doctrine of original sin, although the idea must have been much older and the seeds of it are to be found in the canonical Old Testament.

The Good Life. The ethical teaching of the Apocrypha is perhaps its finest achievement. Certain passages in Ecclesiasticus and Tobit strike us as very close to the Sermon on the Mount, although there are many things, especially in Ecclesiasticus, which are certainly far below it. The ethical ideas of Tobit stand more than halfway between the Old Testament and the New, and in its pronouncement of the negative golden rule (4: 15) the book falls just short of the New Testament standard. Unfortunately, we also note a certain superficiality of thought, both in Tobit and Ben Sira, which leads to overemphasis on the giving of alms as the supreme act of religious devotion. In Judaism of New Testament times, the word *righteousness* actually came to be a technical term for *almsgiving,* a fact which helps one understand why our Lord was so emphatic in warning his disciples to give alms only in the proper spirit (*Matt.* 6: 2-4).

The Life of Prayer. Finally, one notices that the atmosphere of piety in such a book as Tobit is very close to that of the New Testament. In view of the increased emphasis upon God's transcendence it seems paradoxical that there should be an increased sense of warmth and intimacy in the devotional life, but it is unmistakably there. The God of Old Testament times, for all His immediate involvement in the affairs of the world, seems more remote as far as the individual worshiper is concerned than the God of Tobit or of Ben Sira (although, as in the case of most generalizations of this kind, some important exceptions can be quoted). In the canonical Old Testament, Jehovah is mostly the

God and King of the nation; in much of the Apocrypha He is distinctly the God and Father of individual men as well. This development of the life of personal devotion is one of the greatest characteristics of the religion of the Apocrypha and is especially manifest in the frequency with which private prayer is mentioned, and actual prayers are given, in Esther, Three Children, Judith, and Tobit. The address of Ben Sira's prayer "O Lord, Father and God of my life" (*Ecclus.* 23: 4) may be taken as typical of one strain in the Apocrypha which brings us very near to the Gospels and the Early Christian Church.

Few would care to maintain that the apocryphal books as a whole partake of the same degree of inspiration as the greater part of the canonical Scriptures, but few who have studied these books would care to assert that the Holy Spirit had no part in them. Taking them at the lowest estimate, they are at least an important product of life and thought in the community of the Spirit, the Israel of God, as it approached the threshold of its great new age. For the discerning reader, there is clear evidence that the task of preparing the way of the Lord was still going on in the period between the Testaments.

SELECTED
BIBLIOGRAPHY

The Complete Apocrypha Is Available in Four English Versions:

The King James (or *Authorized*) *Version.* This can be secured either separately or as an integral part of the King James Bible.

The Revised Version. This is included in some editions of the (English) Revised Version of the Bible, published by the English University Presses, and is also included in some editions of the American Standard Version of the Bible, published by Thomas Nelson and Sons, New York. It can also be obtained separately in "The World's Classics" series, published by the Oxford University Press.

An American Translation. This modern-speech version by Professor E. J. Goodspeed can be obtained as a separate volume and is also included as an integral part of *The Complete Bible: An American Translation.* It is published by the University of Chicago Press.

The Revised Standard Version. Published both as a separate volume and as part of the whole Bible by Thomas Nelson & Sons. The Oxford University Press publishes an *Annotated Apocrypha* in this version which is, perhaps, the most useful edition of all.

Books Dealing with the Whole Apocrypha

R. H. Charles (ed.), *The Apocrypha and Pseudepigrapha of the Old Testament* (New York: Oxford, 1913). A standard and exhaustive work in two large volumes, containing text, introduction and commentary on all the Apocrypha and the most important Pseudepigrapha.

R. H. Pfeiffer, *History of New Testament Times with an Introduction to the Apocrypha* (New York: Harper, 1949). A comprehensive and rather technical book, including a thorough and competent history of the events and tendencies of the inter-testamental period as well as a detailed discussion of the books of the Apocrypha and many of the Pseudepigrapha. An invaluable contemporary reference work.

W. O. E. Oesterley, *An Introduction to the Books of the Apocrypha* (New York: Macmillan, 1935). A standard work, less exhaustive than the preceding. It does not deal with the Pseudepigrapha.

C. C. Torrey, *The Apocryphal Literature: A Brief Introduction* (New Haven: Yale University Press, 1945). Important as finally gathering into one book the opinions and original conclusions of a great scholar in the field. Includes the Pseudepigrapha.

E. J. Goodspeed, *The Story of the Apocrypha* (Chicago: University of Chicago Press, 1939). A brief and very readable study for the general reader, by the modern translator of the Apocrypha.

B. M. Metzger, *An Introduction to the Apocrypha* (New York: Oxford University Press, 1957). A readable book for the general reader, produced in connection with the RSV mentioned above.

L. H. Brockington, *A Critical Introduction to the Apocrypha* (London: Duckworth, 1961). Brief, moderately technical, for theological students.

Brief articles, introductions, and commentaries are to be found in C. Gore (ed.), *A New Commentary on Holy Scripture* (New York: Macmillan, 1929), and in W. K. Lowther Clarke, *Concise Bible Commentary* (New York: Macmillan, 1953). Excellent up-to-date articles on all the books, personalities, and historical and literary problems of the Apocrypha will be found in *The Interpreter's Dictionary of the Bible,* four volumes (New York and Nashville: Abingdon Press, 1962). Commentaries on the Apocryphal books are also included in *The Interpreter's One Volume Bible Commentary* (Abingdon, 1969).

Books on the Religious, Political and Cultural History of the Inter-testamental Period

Josephus, *Jewish Antiquities* and *The Jewish War,* translated by H. S. J. Thackeray and R. Marcus in the "Loeb Classical Library" (Cambridge: Harvard University Press). The final volume of the *Antiquities* has not yet appeared. *The Jewish War* is also published in "Everyman's Library" (New York: Dutton).

R. H. Pfeiffer, *History of New Testament Times* (see above).

Emil Schürer, *A History of the Jewish People in the Time of Jesus Christ* (New York: Scribner). The standard work, in five volumes. This translation into English is out-of-date in many particulars; the German original has been revised.

W. O. E. Oesterley and T. H. Robinson, *A History of Israel* (Oxford: 1932). Volume II of this basic English reference text covers the period 586 B.C. to A.D. 135.

G. H. Box, *Judaism in the Greek Period* (Oxford: 1932). One of the volumes in the "Clarendon Bible." Partly history, partly Bible text (Canonical Old Testament and Apocrypha), and partly commentary. Somewhat fragmentary, but useful. Intended for the intelligent lay person.

W. O. E. Oesterley, *The Jews and Judaism during the Greek Period* (London: S.P.C.K., 1941). A manual on the political history and religious ideas of the time.

R. H. Charles, *Religious Development Between the Old and New Testaments* (New York: Henry Holt, n.d.). A brief, popular manual by one of the great scholars in the field; part of the "Home University Library."

N. H. Snaith, *The Jews from Cyrus to Herod* (New York and Nashville: Abingdon Press, 1956). A fairly comprehensive survey of both the history and the intellectual and social movements of the period.

L. E. Toombs, *The Threshold of Christianity: Between the Testaments* (Philadelphia: Westminster Press, 1960). Both this and the following item are brief, readable, authoritative surveys which include some discussion of the Dead Sea Scrolls; intended for the layman.

D. S. Russell, *Between the Testaments* (Philadelphia: Muhlenburg Press, 1960).

Commentaries on Particular Books of the Apocrypha

II ESDRAS

G. H. Box, *The Ezra-Apocalypse* (London: Pitman, 1912).
W. O. E. Oesterley, *II Esdras* in the "Westminster Commentaries" (London, 1933).

TOBIT

F. Zimmermann, *The Book of Tobit* in the "Jewish Apocryphal Literature" series (New York: Harper & Row, 1958).

WISDOM OF SOLOMON

J. A. F. Gregg, *The Wisdom of Solomon* in the "Cambridge Bible for Schools and Colleges" (Cambridge: 1909).
A. T. S. Goodrick, *The Book of Wisdom* in the "Oxford Church Bible Commentary" (New York: Macmillan, 1913).
J. Reider, *The Book of Wisdom* in the "Jewish Apocryphal Literature" series (New York: Harper, 1957).

ECCLESIASTICUS

W. O. E. Oesterley, *Ecclesiasticus* in the "Cambridge Bible for Schools and Colleges" (Cambridge: 1912).

Y. Yadin, *The Ben Sira Scroll from Masada* (Jerusalem: Israel Exploration Society, 1965).

I MACCABEES

S. Tedesche and S. Zeitlin, *The First Book of Maccabees* in "Jewish Apocryphal Literature" (New York: Harper, 1950).

J. C. Dancy, *A Commentary on I Maccabees* (Oxford: Basil Blackwell, 1954).

II MACCABEES

S. Zeitlin and S. Tedesche, *The Second Book of Maccabees* in the "Jewish Apocryphal Literature" series (New York: Harper, 1954).

PSEUDEPIGRAPHA

The "Jewish Apocryphal Literature" series mentioned above also includes commentaries on *Aristeas to Philocrates* (1951) and *The Third and Fourth Books of Maccabees* (1953), both by M. Hadas. As in other volumes of the series, the Greek text is included.

CHRONOLOGICAL TABLE

The Books of the Apocrypha listed in their probable historical sequence. (The Apocryphal books are italicized; the books of the canonical Scriptures are in roman letters.)

333 B.C. Alexander the Great overthrows the Persian Empire and establishes Greek rule throughout the Near East.

323 B.C. Alexander dies and his newly founded empire breaks up into a series of rival Greek kingdoms. Palestine comes under the rule of the Ptolemies in Egypt.

285-246 B.C. Reign of Ptolemy II Philadelphus. The Legend of the Seventy Translators. The Old Testament begins to be translated into Greek.

246-198 B.C. Reigns of Ptolemies III, IV, and V.
I Esdras (an early Greek version of Ezra plus small parts of Chronicles and Nehemiah. These books had been written in Hebrew shortly before this time).

198 B.C. Antiochus III conquers Palestine and adds it to the Seleucid Empire.
Ecclesiasticus
Tobit

175-163 B.C. Reign of Antiochus IV Epiphanes.

168 B.C. Antiochus begins his persecution of the Jews.

165 B.C. Judas Maccabeus rededicates the Temple (Feast of Hanukkah).
Daniel (165 B.C.) The additions found in the Septuagint, *Three Holy Children, Susanna,* and *Bel and the Dragon* were made sometime between this date and c. 50 B.C.

160 B.C. Death of Judas Maccabeus.

160-142 B.C. High Priesthood of Jonathan.

142-134 B.C. High Priesthood of Simon.

134-104 B.C. High Priesthood of John Hyrcanus.
Judith
Esther (the Apocryphal additions were made when the book was translated into Greek).

104-63 B.C. Aristobulus I, Alexander Jannaeus, Alexandra, and Aristobulus II.

I Maccabees

II Maccabees

Baruch(?), *Epistle of Jeremy*(?), *Prayer of Manasses*(?). Even a relative date for these books is pure conjecture; some scholars date Baruch after A.D. 70.

Wisdom of Solomon (sometimes dated as late as the early first century A.D.).

63 B.C. Palestine becomes part of the Roman Empire.

The Birth of Jesus Christ.

C. A.D. 50 The Beginning of the New Testament.

A.D. 70 The Romans destroy Jerusalem and the Temple.

Revelation (probably written in the reign of Domitian C. A.D. 95).

II Esdras

A.D. 100-300 *II Esdras* 1-2 and 15-16 added to the original book.

INDEX

"Abomination of desolation," 30, 65
Achior, the Ammonite, 57, 58
After-life, 86, 107f; see also Immortality; Resurrection
Alcimus, 66
Alexander Balas, 67
Alexander the Great, 3, 23-26, 64f
Alexander Jannaeus, 34
Alexandra, Queen, 34
Alexandria, 7, 8, 11, 12, 26, 27, 28, 61, 84
Alexandrian, age, 10; canon, see canon Alexandrian; Judaism, see Judaism, Hellenistic; library, 9
Almsgiving, 52, 54, 55, 82, 110
Ammonites, 22, 57
Angels and demons, 42, 51, 52, 54, 55, 63, 71, 74, 96, 105f; see also Asmodeus, Raphael, Uriel
Antioch, 26, 28, 29
Antiochus III, "the Great," 28
Antiochus IV, Epiphanes, 29ff, 32, 33, 34, 61, 64, 65, 66, 72, 74, 90
Antiochus VI, 68
Apocalyptic, 5, 91, 92, 108f; see also II Esdras; definition, 93f
Apocrypha, after Jerome, 17-21; definition, 5-12 (esp. 11), 18; doctrine as based on the, 1f, 19, 20; contents of English, 12; inspiration of, 21, 111; integral to the Christian Bible, 4, 19; origin of term, 16; use in worship, 20; value, 1-5
Aquila, 15
Aramic language, 3, 8, 13, 16, 55, 77
Aristeas, 9, 10, 14, 27; to Philocrates (The Letter of . . .), 9, 11, 21n
Aristobulus I, 34, 68
Aristobulus II, 34
Artaxerxes, 43
Asmodeus, 51
Assideans (Hasideans, Chasidim), 32, 65, 66, 69, 103
Assyria, Assyrians, 3, 23, 51, 56, 60
Azarias, in Daniel, 39; in Tobit, 52, 53, 54

Baal, 41
Babylon, Babylonia, Babylonians, 3, 22, 23, 37, 41, 42
Babylonian Exile, 6, 37, 39f, 41, 90, 96
Baruch, 90, 91, 94; Book of, 20n, 106; II Book of, 92
Bel and the Dragon, 36, 41ff, 47
Benedicite, 20, 40
Benedictus es, 20, 40
Ben Sirach, see Jesus ben Sirach
Benton, Thomas Hart, 39
Bethulia, 57
Bible Societies, 19
Book of Common Prayer, 14n, 20, 20n, 40
Botticelli, 61

Canon of Scripture, 6n, 11; Alexandrian (Greek), 11, 12, 15, 17; Palestinian, 11f; of the Reformed Churches, 17-19; Roman Catholic, 17f
Casleu (Chislev), 71
Chasidim, see Assideans
Church, early, 8, 12f, 73, 86; Episcopal, 1, 19f; reformed, 18
Conversion, forcible, 33, 35
Corinth, 7
Cyrus, 41

Damascus, 34
Damasus, Pope, 15
Daniel, 38, 39, 41, 42, 43, 94
Darius, 23, 46
Dead Sea Scrolls, 103
Demetrius, Ptolemy's librarian, 9; I, King of Syria, 67; II, 68
Demons, see Angels
Deuterocanonical books, 17
Diadochi, 26
Diaspora, 7
Dietary laws, 59, 60, 72
Dog, Tobias's, 52
Domitian, 97
Donatello, 61

King, as title of high priest, 34, 68
Kingdom of God, see God, Kingdom of
Kingdoms, I-IV, 18

Law, the, 9f, 14, 28, 30, 80f, 82, 91, 106f
Logos, 88, 106
Luther, Martin, 17
LXX, meaning, 9
Lysias, 66

Maccabean Revolt, 31f, 62-75
Maccabee, meaning of name, 31
Maccabees, 4, 5, I Macc., 20n, 23, 25, 30, 31, 33, 62-69, 102, 103, 107; II Macc., 19, 31, 33, 63, 70-74, 102, 103, 105, 107; III and IV Macc., 74f
Manasses, The Prayer of, 12, 17, 44, 92, 97
Mariamne, 35
Martyrs, Martyrdom, 72, 73, 75
Mattathias, 31, 63, 64, 65
Merchant of Venice, 39
Messiah, 93, 99, 100, 108
Michael, 106
Miracles, 69, 70, 75, 103
Modin, 31
Mordecai (Mardocheus), 48

Natural theology, 89
Nebuchadnezzar, 3, 39, 56, 57, 61
Nehemiah, 2, 22, 23, 25, 28
New Testament, definition of, 6
Nicanor, 70, 74
Nicanor's Day, 74
Nineveh, 53, 54

Old Latin Version, 15, 16
Old Testament, definition of, 5f
Original sin, 98, 109

Pacifism, 32, 65, 66, 103
Paganism, struggle against, 5, 41, 43, 84, 89
Palestinian canon, see Canon
Paralipomenon I, and II, 18, 43
Parthians, 66

Paul, St., 7, 77, 89, 106f
Pentateuch, 12, 28
Persecution, religious, 31, 55, 65, 72, 75, 93
Persia, Persian, 3, 23, 24, 41, 45
Personal religion, 55, 110f
Pharisees, 32, 34, 38, 63, 65, 69, 72, 74, 83, 103, 106
Philippi, 7
Philistines, 22
Philo Judaeus, 8, 88
Political history of period, summary, 102
Pompey, 34
Prayer, 39f, 48, 51f, 53, 58, 59, 60f, 91, 92; for the dead, 19, 74; life of, 110f
Prayer of Manasses, see Manasses, The Prayer of
Pseudepigrapha, 21n, 74f, 92
Ptolemaic Empire, 25-28, 29
Ptolemy I, 26
Ptolemy II Philadelphus, 9f, 26; IV, 75; V, 28

Rabbi, see Scribe
Rages, 51
Raguel, 53
Raphael, 51, 52, 53, 54
Reformation, 17f
Religious freedom, 32
Resurrection, 63, 69, 71, 72f, 86, 99, 108; see also After-life, Immortality
Roman Empire, 3, 32, 34f, 67, 99f, 102, 103, 104
Rome, 4, 7

Sabbath, 30
Sadducees, 63, 69, 82, 103, 107
Salathiel, 95-99, 107
Samaritans, 6f
Sara, 51, 53
Sayers, Dorothy, 41
Scribe, scribes, 5, 80, 106
Sects and Parties, 103f; see Pharisee, Sadducees, Zealots, Assideans, Sicarii